Raising Everyday Heroes

Raising Everyday Heroes

Parenting Children to Be Self-Reliant

Elisa Medhus, M.D.

BEYOND
WORDS
Publishing
I N C

Beyond Words Publishing, Inc.
20827 N.W. Cornell Road, Suite 500
Hillsboro, Oregon 97124-9808
503-531-8700

Editor: Laura Foster
Managing editors: Julie Steigerwaldt and Beth Caldwell Hoyt
Proofreader: Marvin Moore
Cover design: Elizabeth Morrow-McKenzie
Interior design: Jerry Soga
Composition: William H. Brunson Typography Services
Cover photography: Dan Lim/Masterfile

Printed in the United States of America
Distributed to the book trade by Publishers Group West

Library of Congress Cataloging-in-Publication Data

Medhus, Elisa.
    Raising everyday heroes : parenting children to be self-reliant / by Elisa Medhus.
        p. cm.
    Includes bibliographical references (p.).
    ISBN 1-58270-096-6 (softcover)
    1. Self-reliance in children.   2. Parenting.   I. Title.

BF723.S29M43   2004
649'.63—dc22

                                                        2004004815

The corporate mission of Beyond Words Publishing, Inc.:
Inspire to Integrity

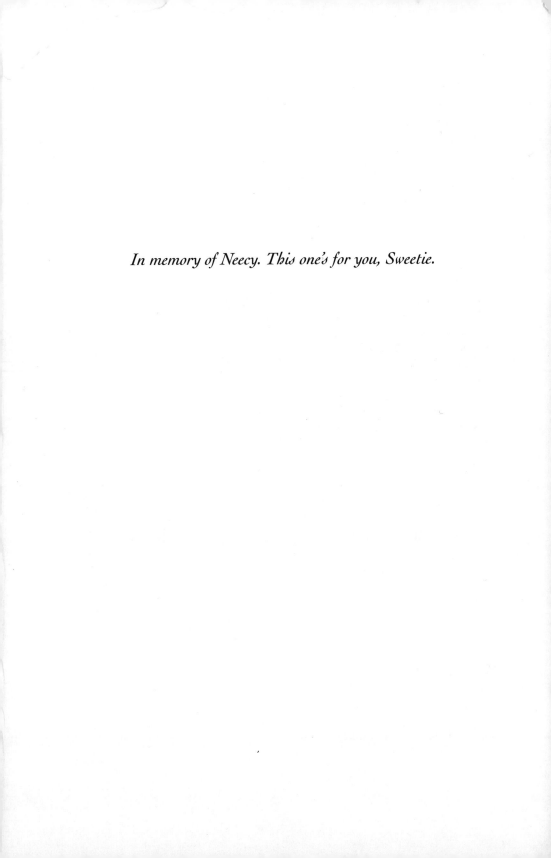

In memory of Neecy. This one's for you, Sweetie.

There are two lasting bequests
we can give our children.
One is roots. The other is wings.

—Hodding Carter Jr.

Contents

Acknowledgments

My warmest appreciation goes to my parents, Jose and Jacqueline Ribelles. Thank you for recognizing and encouraging the hero within me. Without your faith and insight, I'd probably be sitting on a park bench picking lint out of my belly button instead of doing what impassions me so deeply.

I would also like to extend my gratitude and respect to my fellow parents. You've all spent countless moments, just as I have, worrying about or even obsessing over the needs of your children. We've rocked our croupy babies in steam-filled bathrooms until mildew began to sprout from every skin fold. We've rushed up to school to kiss and blow jungle-gym-inflicted boo-boos. We've crawled on hands and knees, looking frantically for that lint-covered binky as if it were the Holy Grail. We've dug Gummy Bears out of the drink holders in our cars, swept up bushels of cracker crumbs, and tied millions of shoelaces. And when our children reach adolescence, we've still been there for them. As our child-focused life passes before our eyes, we've clutched the dashboards of the two-ton steel missiles our brand-new teenage drivers seem to aim at every mailbox and pedestrian. We've endured breakups and breakouts, bad dates and no dates, and everything in between.

I thank you from the depths of my heart and soul for wanting to be the best possible parent for your child, because as you and I both know, there is no job we'll treasure more. No job bears greater consequence to humanity's future. No job is more deserving of our blood, our sweat, and our tears.

My warmest appreciation to all those who worked so tirelessly to transform this project from rock to diamond: To Laura Foster, Supreme Commander of the Editing Universe, I am so deeply grateful not only for your expertise and professionalism but also for your willingness to offer advice whenever I've careened off-course like a runaway train, as I'm so often inclined to do. To Cindy Black, my very patient publisher who must suffer the barrage of anxiety-laden e-mails and hold hands with an author who is still on the uphill side of the learning curve. To Marvin Moore, Elizabeth Morrow-McKenzie, Bill Brunson, Sylvia Hayse, Richard Cohn, Jenefer Angell, Julie Steigerwaldt: without you, this book would not be what it is now.

I would also like to extend my deepest admiration for those experts in the field who so willingly gave their insights and expertise: George Dehne, Alfie Kohn, Claire Raines, Diana Zuckerman, Pete Hinojosa, Gwen Francis, Virginia Leiker, Diana Haskins, Vivian Eberhard, Linda Reed, Wendy Andreen, Winona Emerson, Beverly McDaniel, Elayne Kuehn, Chief Chuck Brawner, Chief Dave Barber, MSG George Pate, Liz Kronick, Annette Griffith, Paullette Hightower, Anna Nowlin, Neisha Saxena, Vinh Troung, Deonnia Times, Kathy Vazquez, Kelley Walker, and all those who chose to remain anonymous — you know who you are! Thanks to you all, together we may well help parents, educators, and children pave the way to a brighter future.

Introduction

I remember all too well the day I decided to write this book. One of my teenage daughters handed me a letter she wanted mailed. Did she not know how to lick a stamp, thrust it bravely on the upper-right-hand corner of the envelope, and carry it out to the mailbox? Or had she just broken her leg and neglected to mention it to me?

Less than an hour later, a seventeen-year-old friend of one of my teenagers loped into the kitchen, all six-foot-four-inches and 195 pounds of him, and stood before me with a puzzled if not vacuous look on his face. After a befuddled pause, he asked, *"How can I get a drink around here?"*

Mind you, this kid has been in and around our house for at least two years. In fact, he's so much a part of our family that he somehow wound up in last year's Christmas photo. During those two years, he's rummaged through the refrigerator, the pantry, and every kitchen drawer and cabinet countless times. By now, I figured the very least he should be able to do is generate a map of each and label their entire contents with individual GPS coordinates.

I found it shocking—sad, really—that this nearly grown man could not fend for himself when he was thirsty! I didn't know whether to look at him with pity or disbelief. So, returning his same blank expression, I pointed out the cabinet where the cups were and always have been and always will be until the house becomes a dig site for future archaeologists, and I told him, for the hundredth time, where the drinks are kept.

I thought, "Two helpless kids in less than two hours. How could that be possible?" Eventually I shrugged it off as an odd twist of fate and went about my mundane daily routine. But thanks to my now heightened awareness, I noticed throughout the day that lightning *can* indeed strike again and again.

My twelve-year-old needed help getting the stapler to work without jamming. My nine-year-old couldn't find his favorite pair of pants—probably confiscated by the FBI as a possible bioterrorist weapon. My eight-year-old needed help picking out her breakfast. My sixteen-year-old wanted a special key ring for her backpack and didn't know how to go about finding one. My fifteen-year-old didn't know how to call tech support to fix a problem with her new computer. Were my kids *that* dependent on me? Where had I gone wrong?

Then I started observing the behavior of other kids—at school, in public places, and in the neighborhood. Over several months, I asked scores of teenagers if they knew how to do things like boil an egg, sort laundry, mow the lawn, give directions, ask for directions, balance a checkbook, and perform other practical life tasks.

I found their age-appropriate level of competence so lacking that I sought confirmation from a variety of experts: teachers, child psychologists, generational experts, school counselors, school principals, and parenting consultants. I spoke with others who interact with young people on a daily basis: campus and city police officers, military-recruiting officers, college-admissions officials, employee supervisors, human-resource managers, grandparents, and of course, other parents. Together, we came to the unsettling conclusion that kids today are far less self-reliant than my generation had been at the same age—in fact, they are helpless!

What was stunting that part of our children's development? Are we, their parents, to blame? Do we rescue and shelter them too much? Are we not preparing them for life as adults? In examining my own behavior, I found myself indefensibly guilty. The chores I had my kids do consisted of little more than breathing and passing gas. And when I helped them with their homework, I'd answer some of their math problems for them—at least until fourth grade, when their grades started to nosedive as a result of my questionable know-how. Yes, *I* was the one who cleaned up their messes, made their school lunches, settled their conflicts, bailed them out of their mistakes, and, well, practically lived their lives for them! After all, it was so much easier than trying to get *them* to do it just as well!

Many of my friends were guilty, too. I know several parents who single-handedly complete their child's book reports, construct their dioramas, design and build their science-fair projects, and write their college-admissions essays. These are often the same parents who bail their kids out of every kind of trouble. Not long ago, one of the teenage boys in the neighborhood wrecked his car while driving under the influence. Not only did his parents argue with the arresting officer, but they paid for the repairs *and* drove him to school every day until the car was fixed! I know several other parents who think nothing of threatening and making demands of teachers—even college professors—to see that their children make better grades than they deserve and get by with doing less work than they should.

From all these observations and my perspective as a physician and mother of five, I've come to the conclusion that there is an increasingly common tendency for adults to rescue children from adversity: from want, from responsibility, from interpersonal conflict, from boredom, from self-assessment, from frustration, from challenge, from problem-solving, and from the consequences of their poor choices.

As you've seen, I, too, have been far from guiltless in what I initially regarded as my own selfless maternal acts of love and compassion. Of course, the desire to shield children from hurt seems a natural, even admirable, intention for any well-meaning and loving parent. Protecting offspring is one of our most basic instincts. Picture the she-wolf that sacrifices herself as she fights to protect her young from danger, and you've pictured every caring parent in the world, including me. Despite its noble foundation, however, the dangerous—and clearly unintended—consequence of this parenting style is that children who are rescued from every conflict fail to develop the tools they need to rescue *themselves*.

In fact, we end up with the opposite of our desired outcome, leaving many of today's youth ill-prepared for adult life. Many are unable to cope with adversity. Many lack creative problem-solving and practical, self-management skills—not to mention plain common sense. Many are reluctant to assume responsibility for their actions. Many look through the eyes of others, especially peers, to assess themselves, to form their identity, and to establish a sense of self-worth, whether low or high. Many abandon moral absolutes to adopt a "conditional morality" by which it's OK to make poor choices if there's something in it for them, if "everyone else is doing it," or if they don't think they'll get caught. Many have an over-bloated sense of entitlement, an artificially inflated self-esteem, and unrealistic expectations for their future.

In short, many of today's young people—currently nearly 80 million strong—are proceeding through life without essential skills or a reliable inner compass. The result: They rely ever more on outside beacons for guidance. So their choices are externally directed; that is, they are shaped by the standards and expectations of the outside world rather than by their own personal experiences, their own needs and principles, their own inner sense of right and wrong.

And there's no shortage of external opinions for them to absorb. Western children endure a continual onslaught of outside messages—channeled through song lyrics, movies, television programs, the Internet, advertisements, peer groups, and other sources. Every one of these messages tells them who they should be, how they should act, what they should wear, what music they should like, how much they should weigh, what food they should eat, and what drugs they should take. In a 2002 survey conducted by Public Agenda, 79 percent claim it is much harder raising kids today amid the barrage of harmful messages they receive. In fact, a majority cites "trying to protect your child from negative societal influences" as a bigger challenge than "trying to find enough time to be together as a family" or "trying to keep up with the bills and the cost of living."

The most disturbing part is not the attitudes or values those messages convey—which may be positive or negative—but that so many kids today react to them mindlessly instead of consciously. They become pawns on the chessboard of life, moved from square to square by the caprice of mass consciousness, rather than becoming players who choose their own moves.

Small wonder many kids aren't able to act responsibly. They haven't had a chance to practice the necessary skills. When they aren't given opportunities to practice in the safety of their homes under watchful and loving eyes, they stand a greater risk, when out on their own, of making choices with dangerous, even disastrous, consequences.

Take a look at the heroes children have today: rock stars, sports stars, movie stars, even villains—public figures whose heroism is defined not by courage, integrity, and compassion but by image, physical beauty, fame, the size of their bank accounts, the length of their rap sheets, and the number of times they've been written up in *National Enquirer*. I find this more than a bit bothersome, because heroes tend to be paradigms of the person we ultimately aspire to become. That said, children today are not aspiring to the greatness that lies within them. Shaquille O'Neal and Avril Lavigne *may* be virtuous pillars of the community, but that's not why children idolize them. They do so because society's definition of success and virtue has changed over the last fifty years. Heroes like prolific inventor Thomas Edison, daring aviators Amelia Earhart and Charles Lindbergh, dignified athletes Knute Rockne and Jesse Owens, civil-rights activist Martin Luther King Jr., and humanitarian Albert Schweitzer were revered for their willingness to take risks and make sacrifices for a greater good; to endure criticism, skepticism, and ridicule; to persevere along a path riddled with failures and setbacks; to do what they thought was right and honorable, elevating humankind along the way.

But now that success is measured by superficial qualities, the heroes our children look up to are limited to those who have any or all of these. Their admiration springs not from character traits like integrity, courage, perseverance, and sacrifice but from this new notion of success.

In addition to parental perfection, we adults are also pressured to strive for personal perfection: to keep our weight down, our skin tan (yet somehow wrinkle-free), our bank accounts healthy, our houses big, and our material possessions plentiful. As if that weren't a tall enough order, society demands we strive for this perfection in an era when time is a rare commodity. We must constantly choose between career success and child-rearing success. We must constantly battle the temptation to take parenting shortcuts to avoid being inconvenienced or over-stressed. To make matters worse, we, too, are up against a formidable foe: the swelling sea of pop culture and media influences that threatens to drown our children, our families, and ourselves.

I'm awe-inspired that we parents have managed to keep our heads above water so well. We should all be declared heroes ourselves for our struggle against those many factors that work against us—factors whose roots, as we shall see, began to take hold centuries ago.

This generation represents our future. While cultural influences are unavoidably and inextricably enmeshed into the fabric of this generation's lives, the question becomes this: How will the culture affect the way our children—our future leaders—make decisions as adults? Without an inner compass, are these children equipped to run homes, businesses, and the government?

Fortunately, it's not too late to turn things around. Doing so requires us to make three adjustments. First, we need to redefine heroism. A hero shouldn't be someone who earns millions of dollars playing a sport and then flouts the law, knowing that his team will always bail him out. Shouldn't a hero be someone who chooses to do the right thing even if that means doing the unpleasant, the frightening, or the difficult? Shouldn't a hero be someone who is willing to climb the steep wall of criticism, ridicule, and rejection that often accompanies bucking a trend, because they know that freedom of expression is an inalienable right? Shouldn't a hero be someone who is willing to accept the sacrifices that many moral choices demand? This definition of hero seems to be the definition of what many of today's kids are not.

Second, as adults, we need to recognize the inner hero—that potential for greatness—which resides in all children. They come into the world with a limitless imagination, an undying enthusiasm for life, and a sense that no obstacle is insurmountable. But over time, pessimism, paranoia, and the ever-present lack of faith in a child's potential begin to forge the chains that strangle their inner hero, robbing it of the breath it needs to do great things.

Can we release that hero from his iron chains, just as Hercules did for Prometheus? This, our final task, is the essence of this book: *empowering parents to raise heroic children*—children who deserve our respect and children who could serve as role models for others instead of children who are the mediocre products of a corporatized, homogenized, pleasure-grabbing culture.

We are, perhaps, the first generation of adults capable of reversing what decades of media bombardment have created. Why? Because we are willing to do just about anything for our children. Our devotion to youth, along with our deep sense of responsibility, our open-mindedness, and our gift for collective action, makes us uniquely qualified to empower children so they can shepherd the world down a higher road.

In this book, you'll find solutions and suggestions that are useful to everyone: parents, schools, workplaces, communities, and even society as a whole. There is truth in the saying, "It takes a village to raise a child," and if we unite behind this goal we can raise a generation of children who are truly responsible, not only for themselves, but for their world.

This huge step will be the first of many toward building a world whose inhabitants are free to choose according to what is right rather than what others deem acceptable. This, a society run by self-directed citizens, is the world our children deserve.

1
Redefining Heroism

A boy doesn't have to go to war to be a hero;
he can say he doesn't like pie when he sees
there isn't enough to go around.

—Ed Howe

As we have seen, the characteristics of the modern-day hero have deteriorated greatly. Until recently, our heroes were individuals who braved unknown frontiers at the risk of death or public humiliation, regardless of the sacrifices. Much of what they accomplished was for the good of humanity rather than their own self-centered needs.

In the past fifty years, attitudes, values, and priorities have been increasingly shaped by a mass-media culture. Quiet heroism plays less well on television than does splashy excess. Because of this, our heroes have changed drastically. Today, our children worship wealthy performers who change spouses as often as they change underwear. They look up to musicians and athletes with rap sheets and drug habits. They idolize movie characters whose talents include killing by day and gratuitous sex by night. They revere those with the most cynical attitudes, the most obscene incomes, the foulest mouths, and the lowest regard for human life. To many contemporary heroes, agricultural advancement means sowing bushels of their wild oats everywhere they can. They seem to live by the motto "Snort, drink, and be merry, for tomorrow ... well, tomorrow we'll meet at my place and do it all over again."

Heroism, in other words, is often defined today in terms of what a person *has* rather than who he or she *is* and what he or she can do to make the world a better place. What these heroes have, of course, is money, fame, athletic talent, or physical beauty. And because of this, they are often given tacit permission to break the rules and sidestep the moral code.

But talent doesn't make a hero, and beauty should not equate to virtue. So before we can raise our children to become heroes, we need to redefine heroism in healthier, less materialistic terms.

Heroes should be people who are willing to sacrifice their own interests for the greater good. Heroes should be those who, day after day, do what they believe is right, regardless of their audience, their temptations, their excuses, the unpopularity of their choice, or the outside reaction it may trigger. And they do what is right for the sake of rightness, not to earn brownie points or special favors.

Real heroes are not only those who risk life and limb to save another, but anyone ready to risk personal loss — of reputation, pride, friendship, confidence, money, pleasure, and opportunity—for the sake of what is right. In short, heroes are led by their sense of honor rather than by the path of least resistance and highest immediate rewards.

I stumble on these ordinary heroes from time to time. The other day, while waiting in the carpool line to pick up my thirteen-year-old son, I saw a seventh grader, Daniel, breaking essentially every middle-school fashion code. First, he was lugging around his band instrument. That alone constitutes pariah status. Didn't he know he was supposed to smuggle the case home with all the secrecy of a CIA operative? As for his clothes, he wore a plaid, short-sleeved shirt buttoned all the way up and tucked into Sans-a-Belt pants with hems just north of the ankle. Those very same ankles were clad in white Fruit of the Loom crew socks with little blue and red stripes along the top. To top it all off, he was wearing shiny new penny loafers. Nevertheless, Daniel wore a broad grin and walked with a confident step, boldly greeting everyone he passed. Middle school being what it is, he was met with name-calling, smirks, and jeers.

I wanted so badly to rush to his rescue and scoop him up in a big maternal embrace, but I quickly saw how unnecessary that was. He seemed to shrug the abuse off as inconsequential and continued to carry himself with pride. And in between being poked, shoved, and taunted, my new hero stopped to help a sixth grader who had spilled the contents of his backpack after stumbling on the steps. Afterwards, I overheard him ask the younger boy if he was OK.

Does this mean heroism requires being a saxophone-carrying, fashion-challenged nerd? Of course not.

True heroism simply means facing every day with courage, no matter how mundane or unrecognized the task. It means doing the best you can with what you've got and making moral and responsible choices day after tedious day. Daniel demonstrated that type of heroism to me through qualities I hope to inspire in my own children—the qualities of the everyday hero.

2
Recognizing the Hero in Each Child

*It isn't more light we need, it's putting into practice
what light we already have.*

—Peace Pilgrim

From the moment they're born, children set themselves apart as very special beings. Who, after all, can resist a baby's smile without returning a dopey grin? There's something about that smile and happy gaze that gives us a glimpse into the child's innermost soul—a soul that hasn't yet been buried under layers of defenses and pain. It's a soul so genuine and pure we can't help but smile back at it.

As children grow, they begin to explore and interact with their surroundings. At first, they're so blind to threats or limits that there is nothing they feel they can't have or do. They know no bounds. But that blissful ignorance doesn't last long. Children are quick to discover that there are threats and obstacles in the environment that will limit them. Sometimes they come by this knowledge naturally. When they reach out to touch a candle's flame, the burn makes them draw that finger back; they now understand that fire can cause pain.

Since, as parents, one of our roles is to protect our children, they often learn through our teachings rather than their own experience. If we see our child reach out to touch that flame, most of us will react by gently slapping their hand away and saying "No." But if we allow that child to feel the heat, the message he receives will be much stronger and clearer. Furthermore, he receives it in a context to which he can relate rather than something imposed on him by someone else. In the end, the child's learning experience is much more effective than yet another one of our admonitions.

Either way, children develop their own sense of what is possible in the world and what is not, what represents a danger and what is safe, what throws obstacles in their path and what opens doors. Those kids who are allowed to explore their surroundings in reasonable safety develop an authentic view of what is possible, because their view is based on their *own* experiences rather than the fears and dictates—rational or irrational—of others. Unhampered by unreasonable limits, these kids are free to realize their own true potential.

On the other hand, children who are prevented from exploring the world tend to base their view of their surroundings on others' perceptions. Some of what they are taught is accurate; some is not. These kids, limited by unreasonable rescue and over-protection, are never allowed to discover their potential and reach it on their own terms. One unpleasant side effect of our youth-centered culture is the tendency we have to take our role as child-protector too seriously. As a result, many kids today haven't had a chance to figure out the stuff of which they're truly made.

Children are inherently capable of much more than we realize. A typical ten-year-old, with some supervision and assistance, can actually paint an entire house. Most thirteen-year-olds can, with guidance, come up with a marketable invention and form and run a company to sell it. Nine-year-olds can mow the lawn. Eight-year-olds can cook dinner for the family. Seven-year-olds can perform the Heimlich maneuver on a sibling. Eight-year-olds can rescue a baby from a burning house. Eleven-year-olds can care for a bedridden parent.

Children can make a meaningful difference in the world. They needn't be sheltered from responsibility until adulthood. All it takes is a reasonable amount of guidance, opportunities to experience success and failure, and our faith in them to conquer the obstacles that stand before the mountains they're determined to move.

Strengths of today's youth

Today's youth possess assets which, if cultivated properly, will help them reach their full potential. Some of these strengths are unique to this generation; others are simply better developed than in earlier generations. Cultural and socioeconomic factors played a part in nurturing these assets. For example, kids born between 1974 and 1994 have had the luxury of living through unprecedented times of peace and prosperity. This period of calm set the stage for a cultural transformation—a zeitgeist of unparalleled youth-centeredness.

There's certainly no shortage of statistics to support this phenomenon. According to the leading marketing information provider, the NDP Group, Inc., toy sales in the United States have catapulted from $22.7 billion in 1996 to nearly $33 billion in 2002. In another study, two Purdue University tourism researchers report that children influence family vacation plans more now than in the past. Alastair Morrison, a professor of hospitality and tourism management at Purdue, cites recent statistics from the Travel Industry of America Association's Domestic Travel Market Report, 2002 Edition: "Nearly one-half of American adults has included children on their vacations in the last five years. One in five parents has taken their children out of school for family getaways." As a result, Las Vegas has replaced its seedy reputation with a wholesome "fun-for-the-whole-family" atmosphere. In men's bathrooms, diaper-changing tables have replaced "For a good time, call ..." messages. Luxury hotels have even become more kid-focused by providing separate, supervised activities and even baby-sitting for kids. Western culture has become a kid-friendly environment rather than one where children were considered either necessary evils or superfluous appendages.

Because of this focus, today's kids are being raised quite differently. In my generation, the typical family was a scaled-down version of a dictatorship. The father acted as supreme ruler whose word was never to be questioned. The mother was his ever-deferential assistant who had to answer to him as well. And the children were the minions whose job it was to obey his commands, to meet his expectations, and to be seen but not heard.

Since then, child-rearing has enjoyed many positive changes. For one, parents seem more involved in their children's lives than before. Even fathers, who in previous generations interacted with their children only after five o'clock and only for the purposes of delivering tedious sermons or punishments, are now seen playing street hockey in the cul-de-sacs with their kids. I see dads at many of the midday school performances, videotaping their children with such zeal you'd think a historic moment was in the making. I've seen them don kneepads and crawl after their toddlers in the slide tubes of Discovery Zone. Fathers are even leaving work early to sit in the bleachers in their suits and ties to cheer on their kids during softball games.

Moms have become more involved, too. When I was a kid, I thought that mothers were born with aprons permanently attached to their waists and that they had cooking mitts instead of hands, thanks to some fortuitous

Darwinian mutation. Their role seemed to be taking care of the household, preparing the family meals, and making sure a steaming plate of chocolate-chip cookies was waiting for the hungry after-school mob.

Moms are now volunteering on field trips, in classrooms, in school libraries, and in computer rooms. They're slaving over hot copy machines, tediously cutting shapes and letters out with plastic safety scissors, and manning sloppy cookie-decorating booths at school festivals. The modern mom is chauffeur, tutor, chaperone, political activist, conflict mediator, confidante, cheerleader, psychologist, school liaison, child advocate, and executive manager. Throw in a job, cooking, cleaning, and mending, and all I can say is "Whew!"

On top of these changes in parental roles, many parents today are well versed in basic elements of child psychology, so it should come as no surprise that today's kids are being crafted with more love, support, and involvement than ever before. Perhaps as a result, kids today seem to have a healthy respect for authority and a better relationship with their parents.

Most kids today say they identify with their parents' values. According to a 1999 *Time* survey, 79 percent of kids look up to their parents more than to anyone else in their lives. And 90 percent say they feel very close to their parents. There has also been a steady decline in the percentage of children who report significant conflict with their parents. In the Alfred P. Sloan Study, a nationwide longitudinal study of students conducted by the National Opinion Research Center and the University of Chicago in the late 1990s, most tenth and twelfth graders feel that their parents love and accept them. Nearly half feel appreciated for who they are and regard their parents as strong sources of support.

Another encouraging reward of our parenting and cultural transformation is the unflinching sense of optimism, high ambitions, and strong self-esteem characterizing this generation. According to a 1999 *USA Weekend* "Survey of Teens," 52 percent feel they will be better off than their parents when they reach that same age. When asked how much they expect to earn by age thirty, the median answer was $75,000. (The average income for thirty-year-olds in 1999 was $27,000.) According to the Sloan Study, more than 88 percent of adolescents who report highly supportive parents expect to earn a college, professional, or advanced degree. The "Class of 2000 Survey" by Neil Howe and William Strauss, authors of *Millennials Rising*, revealed that 77 percent of kids are either very or somewhat confident about their future. If their optimism and self-confidence are justified, these attitudes will serve them well as adults.

Young people have also been altered, in part, by the globalization of economies and the cultural diversity that followed in its wake. Many live in nontraditional households—same-sex parents, single parents, mixed-race parents, multigenerational families, and so on. As a result, they are perhaps the most diversity-tolerant generation ever. When asked in a 1999 *Reaction.com* poll, 82 percent of teens report that they are completely comfortable dating someone from a different race. In a 1999 *Time* survey of six- to fourteen-year-olds, 90 percent claim to have friends of another race.

As babies born into the Digital Age, no other generation has demonstrated the same level of technological know-how. Whenever my computer has a tantrum, I no longer panic or rhythmically bang my head against the monitor, because being the techno-wizards they are, my kids can always come to the rescue. In fact, one of the perks to being a parent today is that you never have to learn how to install software, burn a CD, or set the VCR to record a show.

Being knowledgeable and fearless Internet surfers, today's kids are savvy consumers. I dropped my *Consumer Reports* subscription because, with a few metaphorical keystrokes, I can at any time get an in-depth report from my teenager's mouth on anything from toilet flush valves to garbage disposals. Today's kids are such expert consumers that many often guide the family purchases.

Computers and the competitive spirit of Western culture have blessed kids with many more options than they had in the past. Their lives are like a Chinese menu: countless choices for entertainment, consumer goods, educational resources, and information.

The baby boomers' idealistic worldview, spiritual curiosity, and penchant for team spirit and cooperation live on, contributing to the fact that this latest generation is more sociable and civic-minded than those of the past. For instance, many kids are more eager to volunteer than in previous generations. According to the UCLA/Higher Education Research Institute's 1999 "Annual Freshman Survey," youth volunteering is up 12 percent over the last ten years. This same survey found that 70 percent of young people ages fifteen to twenty-one have at some point in their lives participated in activities to help strengthen their community. A 1998 "Teenage Marketing and Lifestyle Study" conducted by Teenage Research Unlimited found that 73 percent of young people think their efforts can have a positive impact on their communities.

Since President Bush's call on Americans in 2001 to devote two years to volunteer service, Peace Corps applications in the eighteen- to twenty-four-year-old group have risen 18.3 percent. Teach America, which recruits recent graduates to teach in public or rural schools, reports a similar increase. Applications for AmeriCorps, a national service program created in 1994, saw a 75 percent increase in online applications from February to March of 2002.

Whether due to improvements in prenatal care, overall nutrition, or parenting factors, many experts think kids are smarter today. According to David Berliner, a researcher and Regent's Professor at Arizona State University's College of Education, today's students have IQs that are, on average, fourteen points higher than their grandparents and seven points higher than their parents. In fact, the overall percentage of students with IQs over 145 is eighteen times greater than two generations ago.

However, as the next three chapters show, some of these attributes unique to today's youth are double-edged swords. An IQ of 235 won't be much help to a person with no ambitions, creativity, or common sense. It may even backfire, particularly in those with little or no moral sense. As parents, our job is to nurture the strengths and talents our children possess so that they become tools to guide them to heroism rather than weapons to bring them down.

3

Obstacles That Hold Children Back:
External Direction

*The thing that impresses me most about America
is the way parents obey their children.*

—King Edward VIII

Given their many strengths, can we parents sit back, relax, and watch our children take on life with one hand tied behind their backs? Before we pick out our La-Z-Boys and get comfy, we should know that our children's enthusiasm, ambition, self-confidence, optimism, and idealism don't always necessarily hold up well to the hard knocks of reality.

For example, suppose you waltz out your front door thrilled at the prospect of a day cavorting around with your best friends, only to be met at the door by a cantankerous mother-in-law whose sour expression and three-piece luggage set can't mean good news. Under this unpleasant new reality, would your enthusiasm survive? I can guarantee mine wouldn't.

This is the phenomenon we often see in today's young. When they no longer enjoy the carefree days and nurturing support of their parents, their positive attributes often crumble faster than a chocolate-chip cookie in a baby's fist. And once that cookie crumbles, it becomes a liability that can prevent them from thriving in the real world as heroes.

Many children today are holding these crumbling cookies, or worse yet, a fistful of crumbs. According to a 2002 survey conducted by Public Agenda, most Americans say they are disappointed with "kids these days." A strong majority describes teenagers negatively, using words such as *rude, irresponsible,* and *wild.* Most believe that kids today lack basic values. More people today than two years ago say that "failing to learn values such as honesty, respect, and responsibility" is the most serious problem affecting kids. A majority, including both adults and teens, says that youngsters will not make America a better place to live. Child and adolescent experts, parents, grandparents, and yes, even kids, report that the flip side to too much attention and ease is a host of negative qualities that are increasingly common in kids, qualities that can block a child's journey to inner heroism:

- Learned helplessness and dependency inappropriate for their age as well as the resulting incompetence in practical skills
- A lack of the introspection skills necessary for problem-solving, conflict resolution, self-control, creative expression and imagination, and discerning the reasonable from the unreasonable
- A poor sense of reality about themselves and their world; the first weakens their sense of self so that they become confused about their own true identity, and the second encourages an over-bloated sense of entitlement that perpetuates self-centeredness, conceit, and an unhealthy need for material goods
- Frustration and boredom intolerance and the inability to delay gratification effectively, all of which contributes to addictive behaviors
- Unhealthy risk-taking behavior as a result of poor introspection skills, reality sense, impulse control, anger control, as well as insufficient exposure to consequences for past mistakes and misbehaviors
- A high incidence of depression, anxiety, and eating and body-image disorders
- A poor sense of responsibility, accountability, work ethic, and overall moral judgment; moral decisions tend to be based on conditions rather than absolutes

- A winner/loser mentality that encourages unhealthy competitiveness; this, along with a penchant for the material, inspires many kids to pursue occupations that promise wealth and status, but despite their lofty goals, they often lack the reasoning skills necessary to align their ambitions with their educational expectations and to come up with a clear life plan for reaching their aspirations
- Overly fluid friendships, a casualty of their over-structured lives and their lack of free play, resulting in underdeveloped social skills such as making and sustaining friendships and resolving interpersonal conflicts
- A tendency to conform and to succumb indiscriminately to peer pressure

We mustn't lose heart! After all, no child has every one of these traits, and some have just one or two. Many children consistently make wise and responsible choices day after day. But the fact that many do *not* may have a significant impact on the lives and futures of *every* human being—adult or child—who crosses their paths.

Just what's at the crux of these negative qualities? Is it genetics? Luck of the draw? Could it be—*gulp!*—the result of poor parenting? Many factors come into play, but the biggest culprit is something called *external direction*: relying on outside sources rather than their own objective reasoning to find direction. Since many children today tend to make important life choices based on external pressures rather than their own internal sense of right and wrong, they can't cope with challenges well.

How can children benefit from the many wonderful qualities brought on by transformations in parenting when they don't reach within themselves to appreciate, understand, and apply those qualities to their lives? To do so requires clear and confident introspection. It requires the ability to consciously filter external influences rather than aimlessly let those influences control their decisions and, ultimately, their lives. These are skills children today do not possess.

Our kids are the first generation to be raised in a media-driven world. This means they face more external pressures than ever before—pressures that, you will see, make it difficult for them to think objectively about consequences of their decisions and to recognize, let alone tap into, their repertoire of assets. No wonder many kids don't develop and rely on an inner compass! There's just too much going on out there!

If external direction is the root of the problem facing kids today—the stumbling block between children and their heroism—what, then, is at the root of external direction? The true source of the problem of external direction is embedded in our most primordial human attributes and can be traced back through the millennia. Yes, I'm happy to report, with great relief, that none of us started this whole shebang. But it's essential to identify that root, because once we do, we can examine how our detour to external direction helped cultivate and perpetuate parenting practices that encourage our children to make choices based on forces over which they have little or no control.

Once we understand the forces behind externally directed behavior, we parents have the power to change. And once we see how these patterns developed over time, we'll feel more empowered and more confident about using the simple, effective parenting solutions recommended in subsequent chapters.

The evolution of external direction

Humans are similar to wolves and other pack animals in that we are driven by an instinctive urge to belong to a group—to feel accepted by others. Behavior driven solely by this instinct with little regard for our own principles and values is, by definition, externally directed. When our internal beacon is so weak or poorly nurtured that it fails us as an effective tool for guidance, many of us panic and resort to gaining acceptance by, in effect, begging for it. In other words, we conform to the standards and values of "the pack" rather than creating and following our own. So, everyone vies for the most favorable spots in the pecking order, and each person is sorted into the categories of "winners" and "losers." To assure winner status for ourselves, all our choices must be contingent on fulfilling our need for pack acceptance rather than on our own sense of right and wrong. As a result, we're sometimes required to cast aside the values nearest to our hearts in favor of those of the group whose acceptance we seek, whether the group is mainstream or part of a subculture.

Fortunately, as reasoning beings, we have the ability to temper our instincts with our personal needs and values. Finding a way to satisfy both our internal (reasoning) and external (instinctive) needs is essential to leading balanced lives. For example, a person may earn acceptance by creating a unique contribution or meaningful role for himself that benefits others and still satisfies personal principles. In this case, the reward of pack approval is a pleasant side effect rather than the driving force behind these contributions.

These individuals are motivated by a "benevolent selfishness" that results in acceptance into "the pack." In other words, they make choices to preserve their own interests. Before you ask, "How can selfishness be a good thing?" take note that this definition of selfishness differs greatly from the one in Webster's, because by preserving their own best interests, the benevolently selfish can't betray their own values or principles so they will not further their own agenda by making others sacrifice in their behalf. Why? Because it makes them feel rotten about themselves. Harboring unpleasant feelings is certainly not in their best interests. That said, the choices which benevolently selfish individuals make are often motivated by the good feelings they produce, and their self-restraint is a product of their desire to avoid feeling bad. So subsequent pack acceptance is a happy afterthought rather than a dangling carrot motivating their behavior. Practicing benevolent rather than conventional selfishness requires both self-control and a keen awareness of inner thoughts and feelings. Even more importantly, it requires a steadfast self-honesty that keeps excuses, rationalizations, and denial at bay.

Benevolently selfish people use this strong inner awareness to filter and process outside cues, standards, and messages internally. So they consider the pros, cons, alternatives, and potential consequences for every choice—but they do so under conscious control, so that the ultimate decision is truly their own. In effect, these people are self-directed—the quintessential quality of an everyday hero. Heroes use the fruits of their own reasoning, lessons learned from past experiences, their repertoire of strengths and talents, and their system of beliefs and values as internal beacons to guide them through all influences in the outside world, both harmful and helpful.

The evolution of parenting practices: from demanding dictatorship to rescuing democracy

Children are subjected to enormous social pressures to follow standards set by their peers and the pop culture. Whether they navigate these pressures by using their inner compass or by following external beacons is largely determined by their upbringing. Before we feel so guilt-ridden that we put our kids up for adoption, we must remember that all parenting traditions, along with the distinct child-rearing mistakes inherent to each, have been evolving over the centuries. So both have become deeply enmeshed in our culture.

Of all the mistakes handed down from earlier generations, two are responsible for the legacy of external direction that keeps our children from becoming the heroes they have the potential to be. In the broadest terms, we make these mistakes: (1) We raise our children to shape their choices according to their need for outside approval—and so they become approval-seekers; and (2) we stifle the natural development of their reasoning abilities.

Sure, some of us are heaving a sigh of relief, thinking, *"Only two mistakes! That's not as bad as I thought!"* But since guilt and parenthood are often attached at the hip like Siamese twins, most of us are probably beating ourselves over the head with Dr. Spock's book—the hardback edition, no less. The very thought of raising our kids "the wrong way" is enough to give us the dry heaves. After all, we take our jobs as moms and dads seriously. But before you phone the family therapist for an emergency session, take comfort in the fact that some manifestations of these mistakes are so common and well-camouflaged, they don't seem much like mistakes at all. It's hard to fix something that doesn't seem broken.

In the next few sections, you'll get to know these two types of parenting faux pas inside and out, and when you do, you'll have a much better understanding of your *own* parenting behavior, the attitudes that help produce certain habits, and the factors that can trigger mistakes. You'll see why some child-rearing techniques foster external direction and its accompanying negative traits and how some strategies hinder the development of skills crucial to a child's being an everyday hero.

You may ask, "*Why should I be bothered with the whys and wherefores? Can't you just tell me what to do and be done with it?*"

Explaining why we act the way we do has to do with your sense of conviction. If I were to advise you that logical consequences work better when a child misbehaves than lectures do, you might be motivated to try logical consequences for a while. But without understanding why they work and why lecturing does not, you're unlikely to feel completely confident that logical consequences will bring about positive changes in your child's behavior. Without that sense of conviction, you may easily fall back into your old lecturing ways. I want to explain why we parents do as we do so that we can understand both the need to change and the way we can make those changes.

Although the relationship between children and adults has changed profoundly over the course of history, those two broad categories of mistakes have remained constant. In their own distinct ways, all traditional parenting practices foster approval-seeking and discourage reasoning. So regardless of their unique styles, traditions, attitudes, advantages, and disadvantages, each parenting era has contributed to the external direction in youth. Let's look at the last few generations:

Until the early 1960s, the accepted parent/child relationship was autocratic: the father was the authoritarian dictator; the child was his obedient subject; and the mother was the nurturing housekeeper whose jurisdiction was limited. "Children are to be seen and not heard" meant that communication consisted of unilateral commands and judgments passed from adult to child rather than dialogue. Clear expectations, rigidly enforced, included values such as a sense of responsibility, a strong work ethic, high integrity, and respect for elders.

One of the significant advantages of this era was that much of children's free time was spent in spontaneous, unstructured play, free from the expectations and demands of adults. This free time allowed children to form deep and lasting bonds with siblings and neighborhood friends. It provided an arena in which they could develop sound problem-solving skills, exercise their creativity, expand their imagination, and hone the social skills necessary to sustaining strong interpersonal relationships—skills like cooperation, leadership, compromise, negotiation, and conflict resolution.

Despite the advantages of free play and serious parental expectations, children still grew to be externally directed for two reasons: (1) They made choices based on fear—of parental punishment, criticism, or disapproval; and (2) the autocratic parenting style, with its commands, doesn't lend itself well to the development of inner reasoning. This parenting style resulted in the attitudes and behaviors of the baby-boom generation. The strong need for approval and the solid work ethic that boomers inherited from their GI-generation parents caused many of them to seek acceptance through monetary and career success.

Things were beginning to change, however. In 1946, Dr. Benjamin Spock published his famous and influential *Baby and Child Care*, which encouraged parents to listen to their children, respect them as individuals, and allow them to develop at their own pace. By the 1960s the Western world experienced a cultural revolution; baby boomers, now teens, had a penchant for testing boundaries in all areas of life, including the family. Their experimentation, coupled with Spock's now-common child-rearing practices, caused the pendulum to swing to the other extreme; as young parents, baby boomers paved the way to the permissive parenting era in which we now live. An overemphasis on listening, explaining, and negotiating overtook our children's need for guidance and limits.

Just as democracy has replaced totalitarian governments around the world, so it has replaced the autocratic hierarchies in families as well. When women asserted their equality, fathers were no longer the rulers. (My husband is still licking his wounds.) Naturally, this was a necessary change to the rigid traditional structure, but without a clear system to replace it, parents faltered. As fathers began to lose their unquestioned power over the family, parents began to lose their authority over their children.

In this anti-establishment age in which authority figures were not popular, many new parents were uncomfortable setting and consistently enforcing rules and boundaries. They strove instead to win their kids' affections by sparing them firm and consistent discipline. In short, they wanted to be their children's friends rather than their guides.

Some boomers, due to their preoccupation with financial achievement, neglected marriages and families in favor of careers. In many families, both parents chose to work so that more could be accumulated: bigger houses, fancier cars, more exotic vacations. And when marriages struck obstacles, many boomers didn't persevere to resurrect them; they got divorces. As a result, 40 percent of their offspring were brought up by single parents. These two factors—a lust for material goods and a high divorce rate—ushered in the age of the "latchkey kid."

Later, in economic downturns, family pressures skyrocketed further. The certainty of a two-parent, financially secure household evaporated, leaving children feeling skeptical about the existence and sanctity of all absolutes. Although this skepticism served as a defense against disappointment, it also bred a generation of kids who were cynical, apathetic, self-pitying, and suspicious of both authority and institutions.

This "un-parented generation," also known as Generation X, wasn't subjected to stifling autocratic supervision. They had to come home from school and fend for themselves, solve their own problems, and handle their own mistakes. In short, they lived as mini-adults. Maybe this explains why Xers tend to be self-reliant, independent, street-savvy survivors who are accustomed to and comfortable with uncertainty and change. But because they were often deprived of the nurturing, support, and guidance so crucial to turning challenges into valuable lessons, many are inexperienced in important life skills such as interpersonal relations and conflict resolution.

Nevertheless, these kids were able to learn from the mistakes their parents made. As witnesses to parents who lived in fear of layoffs and pay cuts despite their job loyalty and the personal sacrifices they had to make to succeed in their careers, Xers recognize the importance of finding balance between work and life. They understand that there is more to life than work, wealth, and materialism, and they aren't afraid to find it.

Those born during the latter part of the baby boom, from the mid-1950s to the mid-1960s, entered the workforce at a less prosperous time and were more focused on family. When the economy once again became stable and gained momentum, many moms—both baby boomers and Xers—stayed home because they could afford to do so and because it was now socially acceptable—even enviable. But the stay-at-home-mom movement encouraged us to become more child-centered, protective, and determined, not only to avoid repeating the mistakes of our parents but to raise flawless children.

Many moms became defensive about their decision to abandon their careers to stay home with their children because of their own feelings of inferiority and the disapproval of some working mothers. As a result, they strove to attain the same social status and sense of accomplishment they enjoyed as working women by tackling their parenting as though it were a career—complete with goals and indicators of success.

Vast resources for leisure, education, and other parent/child activities along with the often over-abundant time to devote to their children helped transform this new professional motherhood into the intrusive and overly protective vocation it is today. The general consensus is that parents today spend less time with their kids. This is not true. New cultural norms demand that parents constantly supervise their children. According to a study published by the University of Michigan in 2001, for children between the ages of three and twelve in two-parent families, the time spent with their mothers increased from twenty-five hours per week in 1981 to thirty-one hours per week in 1997; time with fathers increased from nineteen to twenty-three hours. Much of this extra time, however, is devoted to structured activities rather than free play. As you will see later in this book, replacing free play with organized and scheduled activities further stifles our children's independence and resilience.

Those moms who didn't stay at home often adopted parenting practices built around assuaging their own guilt. I know a number of working parents who try to make up for the lack of time spent with their kids by handing them an occasional hundred-dollar bill, showering them with expensive gifts, or being too lenient in their discipline. Whenever the guilt-o-meter hits new highs, so does the indulgent and permissive parenting.

From the 1990s to the present, this heightened youth-centeredness, the high degree of parental involvement, the democratic nature of the parent/child relationship, and the ever-growing competitiveness in our culture combined to give children many advantages without the guidance to truly profit by them.

The reluctance of many parents to exert authority over their children and their desire to be friends with them has robbed some parents of the power to guide and set limits. Many mistakenly believe that a disciplining parent is an unreasonable tyrant.

This permissiveness, often exacerbated by guilt over increased work obligations, has encouraged parents to spoil their children. In divorced families, this tendency can be even stronger because some children learn to pit one parent against the other to get what they want and because discipline is looked upon as an unpleasant task that might earn one parent a reputation as the "bad guy."

Lastly, the frenetic, stuck-on-fast-forward pace of life today leaves many parents with little time or energy to discipline consistently or to wait patiently while their children take care of their responsibilities and practice new skills. They vacillate from being their children's manager to running as a candidate for the "most popular person in my child's life" campaign. Autocratic commands, ultimatums, and judgments have been replaced by soft "discipline" like negotiations, pleading, and explanations. Clearly, neither extreme works effectively.

As the differences between Xers and today's children suggest, neither coddling nor neglecting children is the answer. They become heroes when they are allowed to explore the world around them and experience life — hardships and all — while surrounded by loving support and guidance. If we deny them these challenges, we deny them the lessons that build character and inner strength. If we deny them the encouragement and feedback necessary to transform these challenges into life lessons, they grow to become insecure, distrustful, and lacking in important skills.

This transformation from autocratic parenting to "hyper-parenting" is responsible for our urge to rescue and shelter our children. Of course, not all parents rescue their children, but exactly what motivates the ones who do? To kick bad habits successfully, we first need to figure out how they are precipitated. Some of the provocations might include

- Feelings of guilt
- An effort to avoid inconvenience
- A fear of being considered negligent as a parent
- A belief that our children's successes are a measure of our own
- The misconception that our job is to ensure our children's happiness and comfort at all costs

That said, many children today fall short of their full potential, because they are cocooned, indulged, and rescued in a world that requires them to have the very skills we stifle by such parenting, including those skills necessary to filter and resist the ever-present external pressures they face every day. After all, the true road to heroism is paved, not with rose petals and cushions, but with defeat, hardships, obstacles, and challenges.

In chapter 4, we'll look at ways that parents often unwittingly help their children become externally directed and explore the consequences of continuing to do so.

4

Obstacles That Hold Children Back: Challenges All Parents Face

Parents are people who bear children,
bore teenagers, and board newlyweds.

—Anonymous

It's ironic that parents and other caregivers—the very people who care the most and put the most effort into kids' happiness—are often inadvertently sabotaging the process in their day-to-day dealings with children. With parents already so ready to bask in guilt about everything they've done (or haven't done) to or for their children, I want to emphasize that the points below aren't made for the purpose of laying blame on anyone. I only wish to point out the futility and potential harm of certain common child-rearing habits.

In this chapter, we'll look at the different ways we rescue our kids. First, we'll examine parenting strategies that unnecessarily rescue children from their age-appropriate struggles. Then we'll examine parenting styles that rescue children from the need to use their reasoning skills. Last, we'll look at parenting that rescues children from objective self-assessment by fostering an approval-seeking mentality.

Parenting that rescues kids from age-appropriate struggles

Children today often don't develop the coping skills they need to thrive as adults for two reasons: We shield them from age-appropriate struggles and potential hazards, even small ones, and we shield them from discomforts, including those they bring on themselves. But when we rescue children from struggle, we tell them that we've lost faith in their resilience and ingenuity. It also shows we've forgotten that it is often through struggle that strength develops.

It's not hard to understand why this generation of children is the most protected and rescued ever. First, we take our jobs as parents so seriously that sometimes our own identity and sense of worth are contingent upon how our kids grow up. Second, the media constantly tells us that the world is full of threats and that, unless we hover over our children with a first-aid kit and install webcams in every room, we're incompetent. Every stranger is a potential kidnapper. Every baby-sitter is a potential child abuser. Every piece of playground equipment is a potential death trap. Every toy is a potential instrument of suffocation. Every public disciplining is potential grounds for a call from the Child Protective Services. If we vaccinate our kids, they're at risk for all sorts of auto-immune disorders, but if we don't, they'll come down with polio and hepatitis. If we sleep with our infants, we could smother them, but if we don't, their emotional welfare is in jeopardy. And I have *no* idea what sleeping position an infant can be placed in nowadays that won't cause SIDS. Why all five of my children are still alive is beyond me.

This paranoia surrounding the safety of our children has transformed the very nature of our community playgrounds. Now they're little more than boring, risk-free yard sculptures that do little to stimulate imagination. Swing sets, merry-go-rounds, and seesaws are becoming relics from the past. One accident on a jungle gym and the entire playground is often closed down. Yet this over-concern for children's safety is considered virtuous rather than stifling.

Our paranoia has also contributed to the rise in parental anxieties over the past decade. Not only are our worries growing, but they tend to be far out of proportion to the degree of actual risk in regards to abduction, fatal accidents, environmental toxins, and malignancies. As Frank Furedi, author of *Paranoid Parenting*, so aptly puts it, "'Good parenting' now seems to mean protecting children from the experience of life."

When I was a kid, my sisters and I played outside from sunup to sundown during the summer, going on long treks in search of the Easter Bunny, making mud pies, letting the neighborhood boys capture us and put us in prison, and reenacting episodes of *Tarzan*. I could have booked a flight to Reno if I had had the money, and my parents would have been none the wiser. Compare that to a typical American child's day today. To help assure their children's safety and allay their own anxieties, many parents have responded by rigidly structuring their kids' lives. The weeks are so crammed with soccer games, piano lessons, baseball practices, and group tutoring sessions that children rarely have an opportunity to enjoy free time playing with their siblings and neighborhood peers. In 1981, the average child in our country engaged in free time (after eating, sleeping, studying, and participating in organized activities) 40 percent of the day. By 1997, that figure was down to 25 percent.

Even worse, we feel obliged to do more than keep our children out of harm's way. We feel that it is our responsibility to spare them *any* discomfort—to keep them happy and satisfied. As California psychologist Wendy Mogel points out in *The Blessing of a Skinned Knee*, today's parents seem to care so much about their children *feeling* good that they often forget to teach them about *being* good. And society supports this by teaching parents that their job is to make their child's hurt go away, that saying "no" to their child might mean they are a "bad" parent.

So we rescue children from as many struggles as we can—challenging tasks, interpersonal conflicts, boredom, frustration, responsibility, commitment, delayed gratification, and the consequences of their own mistakes. I've certainly been guilty of every one of these. I don't know how many times I've sighed and loaded their dirty dishes in the dishwasher, picked up their toys and dirty clothes littering the floor, settled their arguments, helped them find excuses for not keeping a promise or commitment, caved in to whiny demands for the latest and greatest, given just a little too much help with reports and projects to keep them from failing, and jumped in to save them at the first hint of boredom or frustration. Of course, I felt this was the very least I should do as a doting mom. I'd just as easily fling myself before a speeding train to protect them from certain death as I would pick up their smelly socks to spare them the nausea and inconvenience.

Am I alone in my "super-parent" role? Do child-rescuers like me represent a small minority? Those I interviewed supported my suspicion that not only did I have company, but I was in the majority! Most parents I interviewed admitted to doing all they could to please their children. Almost everyone confessed to some if not most of the following conduct with their children:

- Giving them few if any responsibilities, including chores
- Taking care of their responsibilities for them
- Not insisting they keep their promises and commitments
- Helping them make excuses for their mistakes
- Failing to give them consequences for their misbehavior

- Bailing them out of the consequences that are either given by others, like teachers, or that occur naturally
- Rushing in to find a solution for their complaints of boredom
- Intervening when they become frustrated
- Jumping in to resolve their conflicts with other people, including friends, siblings, and adults
- Giving in to their demands for immediate gratification
- Buying them things we can barely afford in order to "make them happy"
- Helping them pull their grades up by writing their book reports, doing some of their homework, and so on
- Intervening when they struggle with a challenging task or problem
- Helping to ensure their success by filling out their college applications, writing their admission essays, spending thousands of dollars on SAT prep courses and educational consultants, and so on
- Going out of our way to inflate their self-esteem, whether they've earned it or not

Other factors compel us to rescue our children from adversity. For instance, today's time crunch leaves parents little time to wait for children to solve their problems on their own. I remember clenching my jaw as I watched my toddlers tie their shoes ever so slowly before I took them to school—the sound of the clock ticking like a Chinese water torture. With the imminent possibility of being tardy for school and also with a waiting room full of sighing patients at my office, it was all I could do to keep from jumping in to do the task for them. (Velcro straps provide only temporary relief, because I've never come across them in the shoe department for teenagers.) Let's face it, letting children struggle is time-consuming and inconvenient. So we clean up their spills, pick up their dirty clothes, do some of their chores—all to avoid the hassle of nagging them until they do these tasks themselves and to escape the torture that comes from watching them fumble along at a snail's pace.

Competition is another ingredient contributing to the rescue phenomenon that hobbles our children's inner hero. Western culture, in particular, fosters a hyper-competitive, winner/loser mentality that insists parents do their best to raise trouble-free, flawless children who have all of their needs fully met. Society often marks parents as inept when their children fail academically. And those parents who don't jump down the teacher's throat to insist their child be given a second chance are considered negligent.

This same pathological competitiveness drives some parents to resort to any measure to rescue their children from defeat or humiliation in sports. A survey in 2002 by Public Agenda found that parents engage in more rude behavior during their children's sports matches than in the past—shouting, shoving, insulting, cursing, and gesturing rudely at coaches or other parents. Sometimes, aggressive rescuing winds up in tragedy, as when one father murdered another during their children's hockey practice.

So what does all this rescuing from life's challenges mean for today's youth? What can we expect from our children when they're rescued and over-protected again and again? The repercussions of excessive rescuing are like a very long chain of dominoes that stack up against each other, only to topple one by one in wave-like procession. For the remainder of this section, we'll take a look at some of these dominoes.

In a culture where children's feelings are handled with kid gloves to protect and even artificially inflate their self-esteem, many children have an unrealistic view of their limits and abilities as well as their strengths and weaknesses. As these children move from elementary school to middle school, this artificially inflated self-esteem doesn't hold up under pressure. The shock that knocks them off their feet sometimes leaves them scrambling to figure out just who they really are.

Self-doubt fuels the growing incidence of adolescent depression and anxiety. Dan Kindlon, Ph.D., author of *Too Much of a Good Thing: Raising Children of Character in an Indulgent Age*, conducted an eye-opening study entitled "Parenting Practices at the Millennium." One-third of ninth graders surveyed chose "very true" and one-third "somewhat true" when asked if they worry a lot. Two-thirds felt pressure to be perfect. Over half said they were unhappy, sad, or depressed. The American Academy of Child and Adolescent Psychiatry reports that three million kids under the age of fifteen suffer from serious depression. I believe this should be our wake-up call: kids today are crying out for help.

This same distorted sense of reality contributes to another domino: the risk-taking nature that characterizes this generation even more than preceding ones. Adolescents in general consider themselves invulnerable to consequences of risky behavior or at least underestimate the probability that a given consequence will occur for *them*. Today, this high-risk behavior starts at much younger age groups than before, is no longer limited to "the bad kids," and often involves more danger. Promiscuous and irresponsible sex, drug and alcohol abuse, smoking, drunk driving, shoplifting, extreme sports, and body mutilation are examples of how kids of this fast-paced and highly mobile generation skirt the edge of disaster.

According to the "Monitoring the Future Study" conducted by the National Institute for Drug Abuse, which has collected data on drug use by high school students since 1975, the peak in illicit drug use that appeared in 1979 was followed, after several years of decline, by a second peak beginning in 1992. Drugs that have shown an increase since then include marijuana, inhalants, LSD, cocaine, and heroin. In addition, the 2001 "National Household Survey on Drug Abuse" reported that Ecstasy use has skyrocketed over the past decade from an estimated 300,000 new users in 1995 to almost two million new users in 2001. Although some surveys report a leveling off, the continuing upsurge in emergency-room visits related to Ecstasy use suggests otherwise. This same survey reports that inhalant abuse is up 30 percent over the last four years in all age groups, up 40 percent among kids twelve to fifteen, and up 29 percent among young adults eighteen to twenty-five. A government survey reported in the *Houston Chronicle* on September 6, 2002, found sharp increases from the preceding year in the use of marijuana, cocaine, and other illegal drugs and even sharper rises in the abuse of prescription painkillers and tranquilizers. Perhaps more worrisome is the fact that the number of first-time users has jumped significantly.

By rescuing our children from want, we place yet another domino in the chain. Over-indulgence has contributed to the materialism that characterizes kids today. Buying and collecting "stuff" takes precedence over emotional, spiritual, and character growth.

Rescuing our children has also deprived them of the opportunity to develop self-control and encourages an over-bloated sense of entitlement. Poor self-control, along with this attitude of entitlement, has several repercussions:

1. Kids fail to take responsibility for their actions and honor their commitments. They tend to make elaborate excuses and manipulate the system to make it work for them.
2. Kids lack persistence. If something gets difficult, they give up rather than try to figure it out another way. Kids never have the opportunity to learn how to persist if somebody is always there to get them out of a difficulty.
3. Kids develop an intolerance for frustration, which has led to the increase in addictive behavior. The tendency for affluent parents to intervene more when their children become frustrated or bored may explain the growth of substance abuse among wealthier youth. A 2001 study published in the academic journal *Child Development* paints a troubling picture of the early and excessive abuse of illicit drugs among affluent adolescents. Suniya S. Luthar, a Columbia University psychology researcher and

co-author of the study, found that upper-income suburban youth often use more drugs and alcohol than those in lower socioeconomic classes. For instance, roughly one out of every three high school sophomore girls in the suburbs used some kind of illicit substance in the preceding year, about twice that of their urban counterparts. She also found that alcohol use rose dramatically in sixth and seventh graders from affluent families. "One finding was particularly troubling for affluent boys," Luthar said. Among seventh-grade boys, 28 percent reported "drinking to intoxication." Lastly, a 2002 report from the National Institute of Drug Abuse claims that heroin use has been on the rise in affluent communities.

4. Kids show poor self-control and conflict-resolution skills, which contributes to increases in school violence, particularly in the lower grades. Elementary-school principals and safety experts say they're seeing more violence and aggression among their youngest students, pointing to a rise in assaults as well as threats to classmates and teachers. "Some of my most violent kids have been in kindergarten, first, and second grade," an elementary-school principal from rural Wisconsin says. "They simply lose control, and it comes out in extremely violent manners." Statistics support this. In California, rates for "crimes among persons" among elementary-school students has doubled from 1995 to 2001.

Rescuing also gives birth to another serious repercussion: manipulative behavior. Children sense our reluctance to discipline them and our urge to rescue them. Once they do, they quickly acquire the manipulation skills they need to take advantage of our indecision.

Rescuing children from problem-solving is a repercussion that seems to affect many areas of their lives — triggering the tumbling cascade of other branches in the chain of dominoes. By problems, I mean interpersonal conflicts, challenging tasks, or any other obstacle calling for resolution. Depriving our children of problem-solving experiences hampers their ability to think critically and to persevere long enough to find solutions. For instance, rescuing children from disagreements with others stunts their conflict-resolution skills. This occurs when we jump in to resolve their squabble with their siblings and peers and when we deny them the opportunity to develop sound social skills by limiting the unstructured time they need. Rescuing children from housework tasks prevents them from developing the practical living skills they need as adults. Rescuing them from responsibilities and challenges contributes to the lack of initiative as well as the growing lack of self-reliance and independence seen in older adolescents and young adults. No wonder more young adults in America are returning to the family nest.

The repercussion of rescuing that most concerns me is an explosion in relative morality, in which doing the right thing is contingent on at least three conditions:

1. Whether or not there's something in it for them
2. What the odds are of getting caught when they do something they know is wrong
3. Whether they can fall back on the "everyone else is doing it" excuse

Three factors play a part in this shift from absolute to relative morality among our young: their poor sense of accountability; their lack of strong introspection skills, which diminishes their ability to reflect on the consequences of an immoral choice—to both themselves and others; and the replacement of their weak inner compass with a strong inner dishonesty mechanism that makes their immoral choices seem acceptable.

"The Ethics of American Youth, 2002 Report Card," a survey conducted by the Josephson Institute of Ethics and the Character Counts! Coalition, also reveals a significant deterioration in ethics over the last ten years. According to this survey of 12,000 high school students, the number of those who say they have cheated on an exam at least once in the last year jumped from 61 percent in 1992 to 74 percent in 2002; the number who say they have stolen from a store within the past twelve months rose from 31 percent to 38 percent; and the number who say they have lied to their parents increased from 83 percent to 93 percent. Who knows? Some of them may be lying!

This deterioration seems to have escalated over the last two years. According to the same survey, cheating rose from 71 percent to 74 percent; theft increased from 35 percent to 38 percent, and those who said they would be willing to lie to get a good job jumped from 28 percent to 39 percent. This all supports the lack of a moral ballast in today's kids.

A survey of students' attitudes about right and wrong show disconcerting results as well. According to the Youth Justice Board Survey, fewer than half of the 21,000 kids questioned thought it was wrong to avoid paying fares. Barely one-third thought underage drinking was wrong, only 70 percent thought it was wrong to carry a knife as a weapon, and fewer than a third disapproved of "hitting someone who insults you."

Although some will disagree, today's youth demonstrate less *genuine* respect for authority, and many show a lack of manners. In a 2002 survey of parents by Public Agenda, 84 percent cite the failure of parents to teach respect to their kids as the major source of rude and disrespectful behavior. Furthermore, even when parents try to raise their kids right, 60 percent say there are too many negative role models in society that teach kids to be disrespectful.

I do believe that many kids respect authority only because the adults in their lives are padding their corners, fluffing their nest, and spoon-feeding life to them in a manner they've come to enjoy—even require. Why bite the hand that feeds you? Those who feign respect are the Eddie Haskells of this generation, whose ingratiating pleasantries mask a manipulative core.

Never before has a generation been so adept at lulling adults into a false sense of optimism about the future by behaving one way around them and another around their peers. I make it a point to get to know all of my children's friends, and for the most part, I've been pleased. In general, they've seemed to be polite, respectful, and well-grounded. Most of them clean up after themselves while they're at our house. Some even volunteer to help with household chores and to carry groceries in from the car. It eventually dawned on me, however, that it was all too good to be true. My kids certainly weren't that perfect! My suspicions grew as I leafed through one of my teenager's photo albums—with her permission. As I looked from picture to picture, I noticed that one friend in particular was shooting the bird in every shot. It surprised me, not because I'm a former nun from the local convent, but because this was a kid who seemed so sweet and innocent that I fully expected her to collapse into the throes of a seizure if she ever heard my husband curse. On the rare occasion when she dared to conquer her timidity and speak to me, she'd do so in a soft, high-pitched, almost infantile tone of voice, suggesting an innocent frailty that made me whisper in response.

So I decided to rely on more than my own observations by making casual inquiries of their parents and other adults who know them well. Luckily, I have a couple of sources who, for some reason, seem to be a storehouse of vital information—they can recite the rap sheet, grade-point average, Myers-Briggs personality type, social security numbers, weight and height, musical preferences, drug and sexual history, and school discipline record for just about any child in my neighborhood! I don't know how they obtain all of that information unless they all work for the FBI or the CIA. Maybe they just have a whole lot of time on their hands.

In any case, I discovered that some of these little angels my children invited over were not at all what they seemed. Although most were "good" kids, none were as innocent as they had led my husband and me to believe. A few even had serious behavior problems at school, a history of drug abuse, or juvenile criminal records. Several were known to be troublemakers at school or home in some way or another. In short, I learned that many kids today put on one face for adults and another for their peers.

Many rescued youth also demonstrate a poor work ethic. The lack of moral absolutes, a poor sense of accountability, a heightened sense of entitlement, a lack of initiative and perseverance, poor conflict-resolution skills, gaps in practical skills, and expectation for immediate rewards all shape the way adolescents and young adults function in the workforce. One manager of a variety store who has been hiring teenage employees since the 1960s complains that their work ethic has deteriorated, and he blames the parents. He says it's not uncommon for parents to call in to excuse their child from working instead of making the child handle this himself. Even worse, parents call in to say their child cannot work his scheduled hours because he has too much homework or because they have decided to take an impromptu family vacation.

Many have trouble dealing with angry customers or criticism from their superiors. They complain about their schedules and try to weasel out of work commitments when a party or vacation comes up. They quit when faced with even the smallest conflict or challenge. They turn up their noses when asked to perform tasks that are tedious or unsavory. They refuse to do anything that is above and beyond their job description. All this, and they still expect to snag the boss's job before their acne clears.

As further evidence of the increasing immorality of today's young people, the National Center for Juvenile Justice reports that job-related crimes are on the rise among eighteen- to twenty-five-year-olds. Fraud is up 10 percent over the past decade. Embezzlement has climbed 63 percent over this same time period and over 10 percent between 1998 and 1999 alone. This generation could prove to be very costly for business and, ultimately, for everyone.

Parenting that stifles reasoning

During adolescence, the capacity for abstract reasoning begins to develop rapidly. But many adolescents and young adults seem stuck in a pre-adolescent cognitive state, unequipped to think about the alternatives, pros and cons, and consequences for their choices. Strong reasoning skills, however, are essential to the everyday hero. So let's take a look at factors that prevent children from developing fully in this area.

For one, children today have little free time to reflect. Their lives are so planned and scheduled that they aren't often required to think much, anyway. More often than not, showing up is all they're expected to do. Within that structured day, children are told exactly what to do, when to do it, how to do it, and why they should do it. Rather than creating and exploring, their minds switch to autopilot.

Moreover, spoon-fed and struggle-free lives don't require the introspection necessary for solving problems and completing difficult tasks. How many chances do kids really have to exercise those brain cells when we solve their problems, settle their conflicts, resolve their boredom and frustration, protect them from consequence, and shelter them from challenges, responsibility, and hardship. Neil Murray, an acclaimed expert in generational issues, says, "Nothing in standard millennial upbringing stimulates self-reflection. Unfettered success, arranged and realized, doesn't lead to introspection."

Mistakes can be powerful fodder for thought, yet when our children do, by some miraculous fluke, suffer consequences for their mistakes, we, with our own over-scheduled lives, seldom take the time to show them how to turn that hurt into a valuable lesson. Problems can also provide our children with opportunities to exercise their thinking muscles, but when they encounter one, we seldom take the time to guide them to its solution. If they can't immediately solve it, they give up, or we take over. If they do find a solution on their own, we're seldom there to give them the feedback they need to turn that success into strategies they can apply to future problems.

Exploring and expressing our innermost thoughts requires strong reasoning skills, but children are rarely invited or encouraged to share their ideas, thoughts, and opinions. And those they do share are often ignored or belittled.

Passive entertainment doesn't encourage deep introspection, either. In the 2000 "Gallup Youth Survey" of thirteen- to seventeen-year-olds, seven in ten admit they watch too much television; 77 percent of sixth graders have televisions in their bedrooms, and 65 percent of all adolescents report watching television during dinner. The Internet also competes with the time we spend with our children and the time they spend introspecting. A 2000 study by UCLA reported that kids twelve to fifteen years old spend eight hours a week online—nearly one full day! And then there are movies, video games, and other avenues of passive engagement.

The media has become a formidable force in hindering the development of our children's reasoning skills. Although we've seen that kids today spend more time with their parents than in previous generations, that time rarely involves emotional or social engagement. Waiting for them to finish soccer practice and making dinner while they watch cartoons or play video games in their rooms is more about geographic proximity than genuine interaction. One study from the University of Maryland shows that American children spend 40 percent less time *interacting* with their parents than they did in 1965. So with whom do they interact, if not with us, their parents? According to James P. Steyer, sociologist and author of *The Other Parent*, the media is "a force that is shaping their reality, setting their expectations, guiding their behavior, defining their self-image, and dictating their interests, choices and values." The media no longer tries to make social or political statements. Driven by the bottom line, its intent now is to shock and thrill—with little regard for the consequences to our children.

Choice-making is another powerful training ground for reasoning skills, because to choose, one must think. But we sometimes make decisions and even speak for our children instead of letting them interact with others or solve their own problems. I remember taking my six-year-old son to a psychologist to diagnose some focusing problems his teacher had observed. Whenever the doctor asked Lukas a question, I'd answer. After a glare from the doctor that could have melted the paint off the walls, I did my best to bite my tongue. The doctor then asked Lukas, "Have you had any medical problems in the past?" After a long pause, which left my tongue with permanent incisor marks, Lukas finally exclaimed, "Well, I do get wedgies all the time." See? He didn't need my help after all!

Furthermore, we seldom give our children opportunities to make decisions for themselves or the family, whether picking out a family vacation destination or choosing the table at a restaurant.

Reasoning skills also develop when our children reflect on their own performance, their talents, their potential, and their strengths and weaknesses. But children rarely have the opportunity to assess themselves, because they're surrounded by judges and juries, whether adults or peers, who take care of that job for them.

Children also lose confidence in their ability to think when we counter their ideas with our own in a way that suggests ours are superior. In fact, whenever their attempts at creative thought are shot down, whether expressing their ideas, making choices, or assessing themselves, they learn to have more faith in everyone else's thoughts than their own.

Imposing our sense of superiority can thwart our children's thinking ability in other ways, too. For instance, when we tell our children what to do all the time, they don't have to think of it themselves.

Reasoning clearly is a difficult task for the novice thinker, but muddying the waters with confusion makes it even harder. And yet we often confuse our children by imposing unreasonable rules and boundaries, having different standards of behavior for adults and kids, and relying on permissive or inconsistent parenting techniques.

When children learn to displace rational internal dialogue with inner dishonesty, sound, effective reasoning skills fail to develop properly. Yet we sometimes look the other way when our children engage in obvious inner dishonesty like rationalizing, making excuses, or deceiving themselves.

Finally, if we want our children to develop healthy thinking skills, we must model them in our own sound reasoning skills, but we seldom do this by, for example, sharing what steps we took to solve a problem.

Now that we've identified the parenting behaviors that stifle reasoning in our young heroes-to-be, let's examine how these might impact them.

One result of stifled reasoning is that children come to regard thinking as cumbersome—even frightening. They may be comfortable with memorizing facts, but when given an assignment that doesn't have detailed instructions, they often fall apart. Many engage in what's referred to as "Nintendo Thinking," a style of thinking that is knee-jerk rather than conscious and deliberate. This type of introspection is generally shallow and ineffective. In one national poll of fifteen- to seventeen-year-olds, only 25 percent said the ability to formulate creative ideas and solutions was important. Kids today don't tolerate chaos, disorder, unknowns, or the lack of structure well. Why not? Because uncertainty calls for thought. As a result, they handle limited, concrete choices like those seen on worksheet assignments better than open-ended essay questions. This impaired ability to introspect and the reluctance to think critically contributes to the poor problem-solving skills sometimes seen in children today. David Hornbeck, co-author of the Carnegie Council's 1989 publication *Turning Points: Preparing American Youth for the Twenty-first Century*, claims that only 25 percent of all students aged ten to fifteen think critically or solve problems.

One side effect of stifled reasoning is ineffective introspection and an insufficient core of practical knowledge. Many students in kindergarten through third grade can't answer questions like these without looking dazed and pole axed:

"Why is it important to help do chores?"

"How much time does it take to get ready for school?"

"How far do you live from school?"

"How long will it take you to finish your science project?"

Because kids today spend about as much time reaching inside themselves for ideas and answers as it takes for one flick of a lamb's tail, they seldom engage in clear and honest internal dialogue. Their reasoning muscles become the couch potatoes of their minds, flaccid and pale, reaching for nothing more exhilarating than the beer nuts and remote.

Strong reasoning skills are vital to the development of other skills, including being able to organize, control impulses, resist temptation, make sound moral judgments, resolve interpersonal conflicts, engage in objective self-assessment, calculate risks, recognize potential consequences, come up with a variety of decision options, and learn from past experiences. Sound reasoning is also that little inner policeman which monitors for and puts a stop to all attempts at inner dishonesty. After all, introspection is a prerequisite to developing inner awareness—the ability to monitor the inner dialogue we produce. Without this inner awareness, our children have difficulty recognizing and resisting their temptation to pull the wool over their own eyes. So an elaborate system of inner dishonesty can take root and grow, sprouting more excuses, rationalizations, self-deceit, denial, and finger-pointing than my lawn sprouts mushrooms after a hard rain.

When that inner police officer, lonely and unappreciated, dozes off long enough, he eventually slips into a deep coma from which he's difficult to arouse. He's certainly in no shape to compete with all the external messages that vie for our children's attention. So what better opportunity for a mutiny? That flood of outside influences ousts the snoozing cop from his neglected job and takes the helm with ease. Creative thought becomes a rarity. Critical thinking plays hooky. But what's worse, inner dishonesty grows stronger and stronger until the threshold for making irresponsible or immoral choices plummets. In the end, relative morality reigns supreme.

There are other repercussions to rescuing our children besides causing them to make poor choices. When their resistance to temptations, urges, and impulses is low, they can't abide obstacles that stand in the way of what they want. As a result, they demand immediate gratification, they aren't able to stomach frustration, and they begin to develop an unhealthy sense of entitlement that can strip both our wallets and nerve endings clean.

So the first step in raising our children to be everyday heroes is to help them develop and apply sound reasoning skills. True heroes are those who face and solve the problems they come across every day of their lives. To succeed, they need to be equipped with an inner compass that is clear, honest, and strong.

Parenting that results in approval-seeking

In many ways, we parents encourage our children to make choices to gain approval rather than to do what they feel is truly right. Approval-seeking does not unleash a child's inner heroism. Everyday heroes understand who they are—their strengths and weaknesses, their hopes and aspirations, their values and principles, and their personality and character. They don't rely on others to figure this out.

The following are examples of parenting behaviors that foster approval-seeking. Some of them are obviously inappropriate; others seem subtle, even harmless. But all of them encourage children to see themselves through others' eyes rather than their own. Not only does this leave their self-esteem vulnerable to attack, it also adds fire to the already intense flames of competition and conformity. These examples include

- Criticism, nagging, and reprimand
- Negative labels and generalizations
- Remarks that evoke guilt, shame, and martyrdom
- Personal insults and angry remarks
- Judgmental affirmations
- Positive labels, comparisons, and generalizations
- Judgmental forms of praise
- Remarks that suggest our love and acceptance is conditional such as placing qualifiers on apologies or love statements, demands for reciprocity, and modeling our own unrealistic entitlement
- Controlling parenting tactics like threats, ultimatums, illogical punishments, and unfair or overly harsh punishments

- Remarks that belittle, dispute, or prohibit our children's own ideas, thoughts, and opinions

When we subject our children to these, they learn to tailor their behavior and choices to gain our acceptance. While this doesn't seem half bad considering the strength of our values and the fact that we have their best interests at heart, once they become approval-seekers, they'll seek the acceptance of people outside the family—including those whose values leave something to be desired and who don't value our children's welfare as much as we do. The approval-seekers we create will sooner or later seek guidance from their peers, the media, and the prevailing pop culture. And because they're short on reasoning ability, they'll do so with little regard to whether these influences will help or harm them.

Perhaps the most troublesome aspect of being an approval-seeker, however, is the constant inner conflict. On one hand, a child feels enormous pressure to excel. On the other, she is pressured to conform—to fight tooth and nail against sticking out like a sore thumb. In the next chapter, we'll further explore the "push" paradox.

5

Obstacles That Hold Children Back: The Push Paradox

If children grew up according to early indications,
we should have nothing but geniuses.

—Johann Wolfgang von Goethe

The push to excel

The desire to be accepted by others, whether parent or peer, drives children to compete—to be better than as many other people as they can. One factor driving this competitive spirit to pathologic levels is the attitude many parents have concerning success. To many, success is represented by reputation, material possessions, social status, career type, financial net worth, and overall perfection in looks and performance. And since youth today are raised in a time of unprecedented parental involvement, they often inherit this same way of thinking, either through parental expectations or osmosis.

The combination of parental pressures with our meritocratic culture, where success comes from external achievement, burdens kids today with a great deal of competitive pressure. Let's look at some specific parenting attitudes and behaviors that add to this pressure.

Parents often encourage—or worse yet, demand—their children to be the cream of the crop by setting unrealistically high expectations. Parents' expectations for teenagers have risen dramatically over the past twenty years. Dan Kindlon, Ph.D., author of *Too Much of a Good Thing: Raising Children of Character in an Indulgent Age*, conducted an eye-opening study entitled "Parenting Practices at the Millennium." In this study, he surveyed 654 teenagers and 1,078 parents of kids between the ages of four and nineteen and interviewed teachers, parents, teenagers, counselors, therapists, and school administrators. His results uncovered several interesting aspects about the attitudes and behaviors of both kids and parents. For instance, as far as parental expectations are concerned, he found that one in four teenage boys felt that their parents' demands for academic achievement were excessive.

Many parents use negative judgments like criticism and comparisons to shame their children toward unrealistic goals. And sometimes they use positive judgments that drive their children to excel in order to avoid parental disappointment.

Because we all live in a perfection-oriented culture, some parents model unhealthy competitiveness in realizing their own goals. When they do, this mind-set is often passed on to their children.

This pressure to excel begins early. In fact, some parents go overboard to give their children every opportunity to be the best, even before they're born. For instance, some, particularly affluent ones, begin to craft their "perfect children" before birth by reading to them or playing Mozart while they're still in the womb.

Many parents today seem obsessed with grooming their children's academic prowess from birth on. Some even pull all stops to compete for precious openings in elite preschools that promise to give their children a head start by teaching them to read before they can walk. Then it's piano lessons, karate lessons, violin lessons, soccer, baseball, softball, Kumon math, and private tutors.

Once their children hit adolescence, parents prod them along an intensely competitive cattle chute in preparation for the college-admissions process. Some insist their children take advanced-placement courses, enroll in SAT-prep services, take vocabulary-enrichment courses, and receive tutoring assistance in every subject where they average a B or less. Many pay expensive professional counselors to manage the entire college-entrance process for their children.

As soon as their children become juniors in high school, the competitive frenzy becomes even more heated, prompting many parents to interfere aggressively in the college-admissions process. For instance, it's not unusual for parents to call admissions offices more frequently than students do. One MIT admissions official claims to have had parents call to ask for the return of their child's application so they can double-check the spelling. Other parents send faxes with updates on their child's life; some even ask if they should use their official letterhead when writing a letter of recommendation for their *own child*! Many parents have written their child's essays, attempted to attend their interviews, made excuses for their child's bad grades, and threatened to sue high school officials who reveal any information perceived to be potentially harmful to the child's chances of admission.

Parental interference doesn't stop after matriculation. Many even go so far as to meddle in their children's college education. College professors lament the many phone calls they receive from parents complaining about their children's workloads. Some angry parents even confront professors and department heads to complain about their child's grades. Many pressure officials to register their children in mandatory courses that are full. Some call to question the intent of classroom assignments. Gary Stokley, sociology professor at Louisiana Tech University, calls this the logical progression for parents accustomed to directing their children's lives. The rising cost of a college education may also play a role in the sense of entitlement parents feel to being involved in the academic affairs of their children.

This unbridled competition is also partly responsible for the over-planned, over-scheduled, and frenetic nature of our children's lives. All our efforts seem to be focused on getting them into the best possible colleges and universities. Why? So they can land the best careers. Why? So they can make the most money. Why? So they can collect the largest number of possessions — big houses, boats, expensive jewelry, luxury cars, and so on. Why? So they can enjoy the highest social esteem and power. Why? So they can feel loved and accepted.

It's no wonder there's been a significant rise in the ambitions of American adolescents. Large numbers expect to be physicians, lawyers, and business professionals, while few want to work as secretaries, waiters, factory workers, or plumbers. In the 1998 "Primedia/Roper National Youth Survey," 81 percent of students in grades 7 to 12 listed "having a well-paying job" as their top goal.

Although adolescents and young adults are considered laudably ambitious, their aspirations are often driven by compulsion rather than desire. They march toward college admission with all the enthusiasm of an Energizer Bunny whose batteries are drained.

After the college-entrance process is complete, kids are often uncertain about which direction to take next. Many high school graduates I interviewed admitted that their focus was only on getting into college, with not much thought invested in which career they felt they would enjoy or for which they'd be most suited.

In this achievement-driven culture, *setting* goals is seldom a problem for kids. Where they stumble is in *obtaining* them—without the complete support of an adult, that is. And what few life plans they do make are often idealistic and short on detail. Many young adults consistently make decisions that are uninformed, starting with choosing a college that doesn't offer the proper courses for their career dreams. They also lack the creativity to research and plan the details needed to reach their goals.

This hyper-focused goal orientation robs children of the time they need to spend considering the needs of others, shaping their own values, nurturing their bonds with friends and family members, tending to their responsibilities and commitments, or just contemplating the meaning of life. In his book, *The Schools Our Children Deserve*, Alfie Kohn describes research that shows students who equate success with doing better than others are more likely to think externally and superficially. This form of mental processing encourages them to attribute the results of competition to factors outside their control. So, for them, competition is an extrinsic motivator. And because they feel they must compete with their peers for a limited number of accolades, awards, and other indications of superior ranking within the "pack," an illusion of scarcity develops. At times this illusion makes overly competitive kids feel anxious, even panicky. Picture being at the end of a long line in McDonald's, mouth watering at the thought of a Sausage Biscuit with Egg Meal. According to the clock on the wall, it's 10:28 A.M.; in two more minutes, even offering them your firstborn child won't get you any sort of breakfast food. Now magnify those feelings a thousandfold, and that's the level of anxiety which competitive children experience. Furthermore, when they have their sights trained so intensely on being better than their peers, they focus on the goal rather than the steps needed to reach it. As a result, they often show diminished creativity, a lack of interest for the task at hand, and less motivation to think through each step along the way—to problem-solve, work with others, resolve conflicts, and so on.

Hyper-competitiveness also encourages children to divide the world into winners and losers—a segregation that pressures them to focus their efforts on belonging to the right group. Ask any child what his greatest fear is, and you'll get the same answer nearly 100 percent of the time: the fear of being a "loser." This pervasive concern contributes significantly to the failure phobia and anxiety disorders so prevalent in kids today.

The constant struggle to avoid being pegged a loser also drives kids to cheat. Trend watchers contend that cheating has reached epidemic proportions, beginning in middle school and continuing through college. In one nationwide study, nine of ten high school teachers surveyed by the American School Board Journal and the Education Writers Association acknowledged that cheating is a growing problem.

Hyper-competitiveness also plays a part in the materialistic nature of today's youth. Of the students I interviewed, 87 percent say they feel pressure to compete with their peers in fashions, hairstyles, cars, stereos, and other material possessions. To many, shopping merits a hard-core level of devotion and effort usually reserved for full-contact sports. That said, where children were once exploited as laborers, they are now exploited as consumers.

Although many youth experts assert that kids today are more civic-minded and eager to volunteer than previous generations, I and others take this with a grain of salt. Robert D. Putnam, author of *Bowling Alone*, a book addressing the growing isolationism in our communities, believes this increase in volunteering may in part "simply reflect stronger public encouragement, including, in some cases, graduation requirements for community service." He speculates, "If this youthful volunteering is driven only by official pressure, without the undergirding of a broader civic infrastructure of community organizations, both religious and secular, then one cannot be optimistic that the increase will prove durable."

College officials are just as skeptical. Many college-application forms now ask whether community service is required for graduation from the high school. Those applicants answering "yes" are then asked to indicate the number of hours required. If the school requires fifty hours, the admissions board looks at hour number fifty-one. This process quickly separates genuine from externally motivated volunteerism.

In short, the hyper-competitive spirit in today's culture seems to have produced many unthinking, materialistic, discontented, detached, and exhausted individuals. They plod toward overly focused yet ill-conceived goals with all the resolve and enthusiasm of a marshmallow. And a marshmallow does not a hero make.

The push to conform

Peer, parental, and pop-culture messages encourage children to fit into a certain mold. This is not a new phenomena; conformity is an inherent part of adolescent culture. As parents, we contribute to this pressure to conform by modeling conformity and encouraging or insisting that our children fit in. Not only our behavior but our words convey our desire for kids to conform. Negative judgments like our criticism and insults shame them into conforming, and praise and other judgmental affirmations reward them when they blend seamlessly into the crowd.

Have I been guilty of these mistakes? Absolutely. Let me give you a personal example. One day my very creative six-year-old nearly left for school wearing two different colored socks, blue jeans with a skirt over them, and an experimental hairstyle that looked like a cross between Don King and a rabid hamster. I cringed at the thought of sending her off to school looking like that. What would her teachers think of me as a parent? What kind of teasing would she have to endure? I ended up making her change her clothes and comb her hair into a more conventional style, all because of my fear of rejection—for both myself and my daughter.

But when children are pushed to conform, they are affected in many negative ways. For instance, it often drives children to dig deep into their own or their parents' pockets to buy into trends such as electric scooters, Pokemon cards, certain brands of backpacks and caps, and so on. It can cost a small fortune! Not to mention the fact that this trend-compliance stokes the flames of their materialistic urges to a four-alarm stage.

Conformity also causes children to become overly concerned with their personal image. Achieving and maintaining an image defined by the pop culture and judged and enforced by peers is everything to this generation. The pressure to be cool is intense.

In addition, conformity gives negative peer pressure more leverage. Kids today live in a world where adult authority is weaker and more fragmented; they spend more time with peers and less with adults. Peer pressure—shaped in large part by the dictates of the media—suppresses the creativity, individualism, and self-directed introspection of teens.

This heightened peer pressure also contributes to the growing incidence of bullying. A survey by the Kaiser Family Foundation shows that 74 percent of children ages eight to eleven reported teasing and bullying at their school. Among twelve- to fifteen-year-olds, this percentage rises to 84. In fact, children in both age groups rank bullying as a bigger problem than racism, AIDS, and the pressure to try alcohol and drugs or to have sex. Although many students tease their peers to go along with the crowd, they often feel uncomfortable with their own social behavior.

Peer pressure also fuels the growth of drug and alcohol use. A *Weekly Reader* "National Survey on Drugs and Drinking" noted that over half of sixth graders surveyed report peer pressure to drink beer, wine, or liquor. One of every three say they feel pressured to use marijuana, which, according to the American Academy of Pediatrics, is twenty-five times stronger than it was in the 1960s. In a survey by the National Clearinghouse for Alcohol and Drug Information, children in the fourth, fifth, and sixth grades say they would be most likely to begin using beer, wine, and liquor in order to fit in with their peers and feel older. Even college students succumb to peer pressure. According to a report by the U.S. National Institute on Alcohol Abuse and Alcoholism, alcohol abuse by college students and its associated risky behaviors are on the rise.

A child's extreme antisocial behavior is often rewarded and therefore perpetuated by peers. A study in the January 2000 issue of *Developmental Psychology* confirms that one-third of very popular children were extremely antisocial—tending to argue, be disruptive, get into trouble, and start fights.

Peer consensus—molded by the fashion industry— urges today's children to carve out and promote their sexual image very early on. Provocative clothing—bare midriffs, shirts with Playboy insignias or sexual language, extremely low hip-huggers—is even marketed to children not yet into puberty.

This push to conform to the rougher, more promiscuous sexual ideation as well as the licentious behavior portrayed in the media is reflected in the increasing use of profanity. According to the American Association of University Women's 1999 report "Voices of a Generation: Teenage Girls on Sex, School and Self," girls cite the frequency of boys as young as twelve or thirteen calling girls "bitches," "sluts," and "whores" or making crude requests for sex.

Because the drumbeat of the media and peers is so strong, many kids feel it's OK to engage in certain types of immoral behavior. Eventually they lose a sense of accountability for their own actions. In the 2000 Gallup Youth Survey of thirteen- to seventeen-year-olds, 35 percent say they are under "a great deal" or "some" pressure to "break rules."

With some elements of society urging them to excel and with peers telling them to conform, it's no wonder kids today feel conflicted. True heroism, however, requires children to be resolute in doing what they believe is right, regardless of the winds that try to blow them off-course. Furthermore, by subjecting them to an environment of conformity and competition, we send children the message that we love and value them not for who they are now but for who we (or others) expect them to be, both in the present and in the future. The end result is a world full of approval-seekers on a perpetual love-seeking mission and a culture that lacks both meaning and depth.

Are we parents setting the right example? According to a 2002 study from Public Agenda, a nonprofit research organization, most of us would say "no" to that question, giving ourselves low grades for child-rearing. For instance, only 34 percent say they've succeeded in teaching their kids self-control; only 50 percent say they've gotten the message across to their child to do the best in school; 28 percent say they've taught their child good money habits; 55 percent say they've instilled honesty; only 38 percent claim to have raised their child to be independent; and 62 percent say they've succeeded in teaching good manners.

In short, although we parents are dedicated to raising everyday heroes, we don't seem to possess the tools we need to have in order to do so. Many of us feel like we are swimming upstream against a strong current of harmful media and peer messages that subverts our efforts to instill sound values in our children.

A world without heroes

Impeding the development of our kids' inner heroes affects everyone. First, those who *do* become heroes can't always escape the poor choices of those who *don't*. They're still vulnerable to the irresponsible acts of bullies, drunken drivers, and high school shooters. They're still burdened by negative peer pressure and media messages. They still experience the changes in their schools that must be implemented to deal with the behavior of students who aren't heroes. And even when they grow up, they still have to work alongside others who embezzle, who lack initiative, or who have no sense of loyalty or responsibility. They still run the risk of marrying a partner who lacks a sense of monogamy, who saps the relationship with neediness, or whose priorities concern achievement that is external, not internal. In fact, our kids are still at risk for raising their *own* children in these same uncertain conditions.

Second, families without children or those whose children have grown up are equally threatened just by virtue of the fact that they live among those children and adults who fall short of being everyday heroes.

Third, children who aren't being raised to reach their fullest potential have a profound effect on the dynamics and welfare of the family unit itself. Such repercussions might include

- Children who don't do their fair share of the work—not only household duties but their own personal responsibilities as well. Parents must pick up after them, clean their rooms and bathrooms, type their book reports, do some of their homework, make excuses for them when they back out of commitments, and so on. This can breed resentment in even the most altruistic parent as she tries to cram twenty-seven hours worth of work into a twenty-four-hour day just to keep the entire household from coming unglued!

- Needy children who try to make it their parents' job to not only see to their basic needs but to assure their happiness. Parents have to resolve their kids' boredom by hauling them off to the movies. They have to assuage their kids' frustration by taking care of what's causing it. They have to satisfy their kids' need for attention by being in two places at once, sometimes sacrificing their own needs in favor of their children's. Inevitably, parents get stretched so thin that they burst like an over-blown balloon, with unhappy family consequences.

- Children who grow into highly dependent young adults. When teens don't know how to perform basic life skills such as asking for directions, cooking a simple meal, or doing a load of wash, who takes up the slack?

- Children who take their families for granted. They can be ungrateful, demanding, and disrespectful. Their sense of entitlement wears parents, grandparents, and teachers down to the point where they feel used and unfulfilled.

- Children who must be regularly flattered, complimented, and praised. Since they don't have power over their own self-esteem, their mistakes have to be whitewashed or excused. And because their feelings are constantly at stake, parents often feel it's their job to protect and bolster their children. If their self-esteem *does* suffer—from academic underachievement, eating disorders, substance abuse, or depression—the finger-pointing is directed not inward but at "the incompetent parents."

- Children who, unable to solve problems on their own, learn to manipulate, exploit, and coerce others in the family. Power struggles hurl the family into a constant state of turmoil.
- Children who, in their need for approval, often pit one family member against the other to seek attention or preferential treatment. This strains the bonds between siblings, between parents, and between parent and child.
- Children who, having grown accustomed to following external beacons, have a hard time making responsible choices without adult guidance. Even as young adults, they require continual supervision lest they make a choice that will ruin their own life and their family's.
- Children whose poor self-esteem results in mental illnesses, substance abuse, or body-image and eating disorders. Each of these can pose a significant strain on the family welfare and finances. Other side effects of poor self-esteem are high-risk behaviors that result in criminal records, unwanted pregnancies, and AIDS and other sexually transmitted diseases—any of which can also sap a family's finances and spirits.
- Rescued children who grow to become rescued young adults. Many are unable to hack the academic workload in college or the demands of living independently in the adult world. College tuition is often squandered, dashing any aspirations for a good education. Such kids frequently come back

home with their tails tucked between their legs, seeking the financial and emotional support of their parents instead of striving to become self-sufficient, independent adults.

Although I've painted a dismal picture, take heart in the fact that behind every dilemma lurks an opportunity. In this case, the "dilemma" is a cause worthy of our focused efforts. And when it comes to taking on that cause, remember that we have two advantages in our favor: We've already identified the root of the problem we're poised to tackle, and we are a generation of parents who, armed by an unprecedented passion for children and a determination to remove all threats to their well-being, are up to that great task. We have our goals defined and our motivation clear. All we need are the tools necessary to complete our mission: raising a world of heroes.

6
Raising Heroic Children

*If you want to see what children can do
you must stop giving them things.*

—Norman Douglas

I truly believe that all children try to find their inner hero, but like my husband and the rest of the male population, they resist asking for directions! And when their peers and the pop-culture messages step up to navigate for them, they wind up on some deserted road in Timbuktu with an empty gas tank and no options.

We parents can reclaim our role as our children's navigator by teaching them how to rely on their own inner compass. All we need are the proper tools—the specific, practical, and easy-to-use strategies introduced in the rest of this book. With these strategies, our children can navigate themselves safely from one difficult choice to the next, day after day for the rest of their lives. Once equipped with a keen inner navigational sense, our children will become true heroes—people who will serve as models for others and who will lead us all toward a better future.

I know the very thought of changing your child-rearing practices may seem overwhelming. After all, life is already so frenzied for most of us that taking time to clip our toenails is more than we can bear. But don't despair, because these changes will make your life easier. For one, you'll see profound results within two to three weeks—results so gratifying that adopting these changes consistently will be an easy task. And when you do, your old ways will seem so time-consuming and ineffective that there'll be no turning back!

The first change you may notice is an improved relationship with your children. They will take direction and discipline without becoming angry or sullen; they will communicate more openly and honestly with you; they will comply with the rules and respect the boundaries that you set; they will get along better with their brothers and sisters and not use sibling rivalry as a way to draw you into the fray or invoke your sympathy; and seeing you as a guide who is on their side rather than the enemy's, they will sincerely respect and admire you. Once they do, they'll eagerly follow your guidance. After all, to whom would you better relate: an oppressive dictator, a meddlesome manager, or a loving mentor?

Parenting our kids to become heroes requires us to delegate to them a large portion of the responsibility for growing up well. This way, they feel ownership over decisions to do what's right or not. How many of us treat a rental car with the same loving care we do our own car? Children are no different. If they feel like their childhood is a rental, they're more liable to leave gum in the drink holders and french fries between the seats. But if they feel like their childhood is all theirs—a brand-new convertible with 425 horses under the hood, leather seats, wood trim, fuel injection, and turbo boosters—they're going to drive that sucker with velvet gloves.

The improvement in your children's behavior may affect your marriage, too, especially if disagreements over discipline have been a bone of contention in the past. No more *"Are you going to do something about those kids of yours?"* Funny how some things our kids do can make us forget they're even ours! My husband used to make this statement so often that I toyed with the idea of hiring an in-house DNA analyst to provide glaring proof.

You may feel wary about how your children will react when you change the way you parent them. I remember how my kids would respond to any major changes in my parenting: *"Uh-oh, Mom bought another parenting book today."*

But most children will welcome your new parenting style, because it is respectful and nonjudgmental, and it sends a strong message that you have faith in them and in their ability to reach their full potential.

Those few kids who regress temporarily do so only because they've acquired clever manipulative skills after years of parental rescuing. Bad behavior in the face of your new "hero-making" parenting techniques is just their way of saying, *"Hey, wait a minute. I liked having my own way all the time. This is new and scary. What's going to happen here?"* It's just desperation talking. However, their challenge to you will be short-lived for two reasons: You'll find it easy to stick to your guns, and your children will realize that reasonable limits are a good thing; after all, they bring security and stability into children's lives.

OK, let's review: Stick with the old ways, and allow our children to run us and the rest of the household ragged, leaving them vulnerable to the whim of every outside influence and unprepared for adulthood. *Or* try something new that will bring harmony to the family, that will make parenting a joy rather than a harrowing experience, and that will bless us with children who behave civilly and who grow into their true heroic potential. Change can be stressful. But we must persevere regardless of obstacles, because our children are worth it. They are true treasures in a world sorely in need of the everyday heroes they can become.

Each one of the next five chapters will provide you with a road map that will lead you to your child's inner hero. The first step, in the next chapter, is to reexamine your roles as a parent. Here, you'll be asked to rethink your time commitments and priorities; you'll learn the importance of setting an example and tips on how to do that; you'll learn to see your children's misbehavior in a different, more positive light; and you'll reevaluate the meaning and purpose of discipline. You'll also see how to apply discipline—not with the rod but with the brain, and you'll learn the power and value of standing at the sidelines during many of your child's struggles. The parenting strategies in this chapter teach you and your kids that, given the right framework, it is easy to do what is right.

Then, in chapter 8, you'll learn how to consciously create a family identity that teaches and expects heroic behavior through the values each member shares, the rules and boundaries they set and follow, and the family bonds they strengthen.

In chapter 9, you'll find specific parenting strategies to nurture your child's sense of self while teaching him to think critically and rationally about the outside forces that will try to lure him into blind conformity. You'll discover when and how to allow for your child's imperfections; how to maintain your objectivity without taking away from the love, warmth, and affection he needs; and how to relinquish detrimental control without letting things get *out* of control. You'll find ways to praise your child so he learns to assess himself rather than rely on others to do so, and you'll discover how you can help him build self-respect so he can do away with his need for outside approval. In this same chapter, you'll learn how to appreciate and cultivate your child's own unique insight so that he can think for himself instead of delegating the task to others, including peers and the media.

"Mentoring Children toward Adulthood," chapter 10, shows you how to encourage independent thought and behavior, with specific examples and guidance for each stage of a child's development, from preschool to high school graduation. You'll learn how to help your child develop a flexible life plan that guides him to become an independent, self-reliant, and contributing adult.

Lastly, chapter 11 looks at the macro view: how the larger community can help us as we raise everyday heroes. You'll discover ways to recruit support and cooperation from your child's school, your community, the media, and other influences so that the challenges your new hero faces along the journey to adulthood inspire strength and growth rather than bring about obstacles and discouragement.

7

Reexamining Our Role as Parents

Nothing grows well in the shade of a big tree.

—Constantin Brancusi

How do you see yourself as a parent? Are you judge? Dictator? Executive manager? Doormat? Lackey? Does it depend on the day of the week? Your mood? The season? Or are you like *I* have been in the past—a little of each all the time?

Each one of these roles is not only exhausting for both parent and child, each is also counterproductive to bringing out the hero in children, because all of these roles reflect a lack of faith. They're designed for parents who do not believe in their kids and who therefore feel they can direct their lives better than the children themselves can. Many of these roles are built on fear—parents who are afraid of messing up what they see as the most important job they will ever have. They believe that if their children fall short of their or society's expectations, they've failed as parents. Some of these roles are based on a guilt that compels many to guarantee their children's happiness and to remain the ever-popular parent. But from parents, kids need guidance, not friendships.

So our first step is to make a mental shift in the role we play in our children's lives. Never again will we be their dictator, manager, doormat, judge, or slave. To bring forth everyday heroes, we will become our children's coach, guide, and mentor. Try to remember the teachers you most admired in your life. What were they like? What was it about them that you respected? I'll bet my last nickel that they were firm but unconditionally loving; that they gave feedback, not criticism; that they set high but attainable expectations; and that they exuded, perhaps subliminally, a strong confidence in your abilities. In other words, these were teachers who had faith in you and who knew how to inspire you to achieve personal excellence without damaging your self-esteem. This is the kind of guide we can and will become. This is the kind of guide our children deserve.

Rethinking time commitments and priorities

It takes more time to guide children toward making a responsible choice than it does to order them to do it, to shame them into it, or to choose for them. So to gather the resolve and determination you need, step back and reexamine what's really important to you as a parent. Most of us see the welfare of our children as our number-one priority. But sometimes we let other commitments take precedence: work, volunteering, socializing, exercise. If you're like most parents today, you may need to restructure your life to include more time to be a parent—to mentor your children.

Finding more hours in the day to do this might not be as difficult a task as you think. Since the discipline strategies in this chapter are efficient and effective, the time your children spend misbehaving and the time you spend trying to correct them will decrease considerably. With less time and energy spent on the unsavory aspects of parenting, you'll have more time to discuss and solve problems together, to share values, to discuss your childhood experiences, to help turn your children's mistakes and misbehavior into valuable lessons, and to get to know and enjoy each other.

If you're compulsive like me and rely on an external brain like a computer or PDA to schedule your life, don't be shy about blocking out time to spend with your children.

You would do the same for a friend or for an important appointment. For instance, I block out one day every week to spend time with each of my kids—a tradition we fondly refer to as "Buddy Day." On this day, I take the child on an outing so that we can have one-on-one time together. It doesn't have to be long or costly. Sometimes I'll take my child out for ice cream or to the neighborhood park. Sometimes I'll take him grocery shopping and treat him to the Slurpee machine there. The important thing is that my children consider "Buddy Day" to be a special time when Mommy has all of their attention. We've even made up special handshakes and secret sayings to use for that day.

Time spent with you is important. But so is time alone or with their friends. Each day, set aside time for your children to engage in free play—both solitary and among friends. When you give your child opportunities to play with others in an unstructured setting, she builds important social skills like leadership, compromise, teamwork, conflict resolution, negotiating, and empathy. In playing alone, she will learn to entertain herself, to solve problems, to cope with frustration and boredom, and to nurture her creative imagination. Solitary play should *not*, however, include passive forms of entertainment such as computer or video games. These are really just forms of escape. I believe that true play, solitary or not, stimulates the imagination and calls for creativity, such as in making paper dolls, playing house with stuffed animals, or other types of solitary diversion.

At the end of the day, create a sacred time for reflection. Sit with your child in quiet. Spend the time daydreaming, making plans, or reflecting on the day's experiences. Encourage him to think about his values, design his dreams, and contemplate his life in the present. Show him how to do this by examining the events of the day aloud and sharing your reaction to them. This introspection and reflection are vital to help your child develop strong reasoning skills and gain confidence in using his own inner compass for guidance.

Rethinking misbehavior

Shedding old parenting roles to become your children's mentor may require you to look at misbehavior in a different light. If you have assumed the role of family dictator, doormat, slave, judge, or manager, your child's disobedience may leave you frustrated, worried, angry, irritated, or just plain overwhelmed. Why? Because when we take on one of these roles, solving our children's behavior problems becomes more important to us than to them. We tend to see any disobedience as a personal vendetta. There have been times when I've thought my kids were put on the face of this earth to either humble me or drive me insane. These roles also encourage us to regard our children's misbehavior as a reflection of our own parenting abilities. The more they act up, the more we feel like miserable failures. Lastly, these roles, being adversarial and unidirectional, tend to invite manipulation from our children.

As judge or manager, we set the pace by which our children develop rather than allowing them to do so in a way that suits their temperament, maturity, or level of understanding.

As mentors, we are still leading the family, but less as a dictator and more as a facilitator of a team, each member of which has much to learn as well as much to contribute. As mentors, you'll still react to your child's disobedience, but with joy, not annoyance! Every time they act up, you'll get a gleam of delight in your eye and rub your hands together in blissful anticipation. Why? Because you'll begin to view disobedience not as a splinter shoved under your fingernail but as buried treasure—a golden opportunity for your child to learn a valuable lesson that will build character and develop skills essential to becoming an everyday hero.

We all learn much more from our failures than from our successes. I remember when I went skiing for the first time as a child. At eight years old, my fears were few and my enthusiasm was bursting at the seams. At first, I spent more time digging the snow out of my nostrils than standing upright on my skis, but by the day's end, I was carving up those slopes like they were Thanksgiving turkeys. Ten years later, I hit the slopes for the second time, feeling completely certain, in my blind optimism, that I would be swooshing past those shaky beginners from the start. Boy, was I in for a disappointment. Perched atop the first hill, it occurred to me that the ground seemed thousands of feet from my face. But since waiting for the spring thaw was out of the question, I gulped, took a deep breath, and pushed myself over the crest. I was so paralyzed with fear that my entire body bumbled clumsily down the hill looking more like a totem pole on stilts waging a losing battle against gravity than anything else. As I descended, I felt a broken bone lurking in every wide and painfully slow turn. By the time I reached the bottom, my legs were wet noodles, and I was drenched in sweat, panting like an asthmatic walrus.

Between gasps, I thought, "What the heck happened to me over those ten years?" After licking the wounds to my ego and limbering up my stiffened body in the Jacuzzi, it came to me that, as an adult, my superior knowledge of the potential dangers had left me terrified at the thought of falling. So I took as few risks as I could skiing down that Bunny Slope from Hell. The eight-year-old Elisa, not giving a second thought to becoming a human snowball, threw caution to the wind. She was willing to take calculated risks—try new techniques, push to greater speeds, and progress to more advanced slopes.

The point is that when misbehaviors and failures are viewed as positives, they tend to be stepping-stones to success rather than abysses of pain and humiliation. Take comfort in the fact that children learn great things by taking the risks that sometimes end in a stumble or two. In fact, we should be more concerned with children who *aren't* willing to test their limits than with those who do. So when your children make those mistakes, behavioral or otherwise, gratefully welcome them as teachable moments that promise to help them grow.

Learning the value of benign neglect

A good mentor knows when to stand by and watch as a child becomes frustrated with a new task, argues with a sibling, or struggles with other problems. Try not to help your child when she wrestles while learning a new skill or dealing with others. Remember, your objective as a parent is to gradually untie and release the apron strings. If successful, you should be able to work yourself out of a job so that, by age eighteen, your child can confidently step into adulthood with the skills that will assure him a successful life.

By resisting the urge to help or interfere, you will give your children a chance to build a repertoire of problem-solving strategies. When you let them deal with their own problems, you send the message that you have faith in them to either solve those problems themselves or deal with the emotions and consequences that come from leaving them unsolved. Furthermore, by sitting back, you give your children a chance to chalk up a long list of successes — both small and large.

When we let our children's problems be *their* problems, not ours, they learn that their problems are never going to be more important to us than to them. This is because we have faith in them to handle the situation by themselves, not because we don't care about our children. Kids have to learn that when they are adults, no one else will care about their problems to the extent they will need to care themselves.

When you give your children a chance to fail, be ready to talk about why things went wrong. Brainstorm with them about the steps they could take to ensure success the next time around. Benign neglect doesn't mean you totally ignore your kids in their hour of need — just that you let them solve their own issues, and then you can turn the mistakes into teachable moments.

By allowing your children to handle their own problems, you reassert that they are the true masters of their own destinies. In short, while benign neglect gives us parents more time to plan dinner and trim our cuticles, more important, it empowers our children and lets them know that they can and will be entrusted with more and more time at the helm.

Rethinking discipline and its purpose

Children are inherently self-absorbed. They come into this world completely unequipped to consider the feelings and welfare of others. But that's what being a parent is all about: civilizing them and drawing out their humanity so they don't grow up to be selfish clods. We can try to achieve this by punishment that breaks their spirits and fosters external direction or by discipline that, in its true sense, builds the strength and character they need to seek guidance from their own inner wisdom.

In order to become an effective mentor, it's important to grasp the differences between punishment and discipline. Punishment controls. Discipline guides and teaches so that children can learn to control themselves. Punishment motivates children to behave well because they *fear* our reaction. Discipline motivates them to comply with rules because doing so is right. And they determine right from wrong because discipline gives them the opportunity to think about the connection between poor behavior and its consequences. Once a child understands this connection, she can come up with acceptable alternatives for misbehavior.

Punishment often smacks of disapproval. And since disapproval is usually expressed with negative judgments, insults, and threats, the child's self-worth eventually weakens. Once his self-esteem erodes enough, he begins to lose faith in his ability to make sound choices. Eventually he'll put more stock into the choices, opinions, and values of others than he does in his own. Needless to say, misbehaviors continue or increase.

Discipline, on the other hand, is objective and non-degrading. Since it focuses on a child's behavior, not on his self, his self-esteem remains intact, as does the faith he has in his own inner compass.

We usually render punishment when we are angry, frustrated, or stressed by our child's misbehavior, especially when we take that misbehavior personally. Other times we levy punishments because of stressful events unrelated to our child's behavior. For this reason, punishments can be unfair, subjective, overly harsh, illogical, and based on unreasonable rules. Discipline, on the other hand, can be more dispassionate, because we are allowing our child's choices to be her own instead of single-handedly taking on the responsibility for making her behave well. The sense of urgency for stopping or preventing misbehavior then belongs to the child, not us. And since discipline is usually rendered in calm, it tends to be fair, objective, and suitable to the behavior it targets. Because of this difference in emotional investment, punishment breeds resentment and refusal, while discipline encourages cooperation and agreement.

Punishment is ineffective because it motivates a child to behave well only when someone is watching or when she thinks she might get caught. With discipline, a child does the right thing even when no one is around, and parents don't feel the need to constantly supervise and hover over their child.

Punishment is also ineffective because the decision to comply is foisted on the child from an external source. Who knows how he'll react? After all, once external factors are in charge of his choices, he is no longer in full control of them. Discipline, however, encourages a child to come to his own conclusion about why complying with a rule is the right thing to do. So having complete, conscious control over his every decision, he's more likely to demonstrate good behavior consistently.

Because of these last two differences, punishment encourages recurrences of misbehavior while discipline extinguishes it permanently. To stop breaking a rule, a child must understand and agree with it using his own reasoning. When he produces his own choice this way, he is unlikely to invalidate it by doing what he knows is wrong. Parenting becomes less conflict and struggle and more guidance and course-correction.

Let's look at an example that highlights the differences between punishment and discipline. Ashley is caught cheating on a math test. A punishment might involve yelling, hitting, name-calling, making her write "I won't cheat" a thousand times, or grounding her. If subjected to any of these, Ashley is only going to feel rotten about herself as a human being, think about how much she hates her horrible parents, or figure out ways to avoid getting caught next time. She's unlikely to reflect on the consequences of her actions on her peers or herself. Furthermore, she's probably not going to spend hours contemplating the steps she could have taken to do well on the test or to make amends.

On the other hand, disciplining her might include more logical consequences like making sure she gets a zero for that test, asking her to apologize to the teacher, having her restudy the material until it's mastered, not allowing any leisure time, including extracurricular activities, until that mastery is achieved, having her retake the test for no credit, requiring her to be heavily monitored until she regains your trust as well as the teacher's, and arranging for her to attend math tutorials until her grades reflect her potential.

She may not enjoy this discipline, but since it comes from a calm and reasoned place, she can appreciate why it's needed. With time and distance from the event, Ashley will see that she has now done the right thing. Her understanding of what it means to be a hero has grown.

Twelve tenets of empowering discipline

To discipline your child in a way that doesn't control or repress, follow these twelve simple tenets for empowering discipline. Afterwards, we'll look at seven discipline techniques that honor these tenets.

1. Establish rules and boundaries to which your children can agree.

Again, if they can't agree with them, they won't understand them. If they don't understand them, how can they produce the internal dialogue necessary to decide that it's the right thing to do?

2. Respect your children.

By giving them the same respect you'd give any adult, you show that you trust their ability to make proper choices. Since you trust and respect them, they then develop the self-respect and confidence it takes to rely on their inner compass.

3. Be consistent and follow through with discipline.

This has been one of my biggest challenges as a mother. For instance, no more than five minutes after I've asked my kids to do their chores, I've completely forgotten my request. So there I am, totally engrossed in reading the directions on my dog's de-worming medicine or alphabetizing my spice rack while the chores remain neglected. I once asked my ten-year-old why he didn't comply with my requests right away and he answered, "Because I just want to wait till you forget." He's no dummy. Kids are geniuses when it comes to figuring out their parents' weaknesses and using them to their advantage!

Because you'll be eliminating a great deal of unnecessary repetition, consistent discipline is easier than you think. When you consistently enforce rules and boundaries, your children aren't left wondering if they're going to be able to get by this time with behaviors you don't allow. By religiously imposing consequences for misbehavior, you imply that you have faith in them to deal with the effects of their poor choices, come up with solutions, and figure out ways to avoid repeating the same mistake. Once they sense this in you, they eventually develop faith in themselves and make fewer behavioral mistakes.

4. Model the behavior you want to see in your children.
When you break the rules that you ask them to obey, you not only muddy their path to the proper choices, you also provide them with fodder to justify breaking that rule in the future.

5. Keep your cool.
Because you're eliminating power struggles and delegating the responsibility to your children to behave properly, this is not as hard as it seems. As mentor, remember to look on

your children's transgressions as wonderful opportunities for them to learn instead of as personal affronts.

6. Give your children unconditional love.
Love them for who they are now—works in progress rather than whom you expect them to become later. One way to do this when disciplining them is to address their behavior rather than their personality, weaknesses, flaws, or character traits. Anything that evaluates your children's identity or sense of worth will only bring on ill feelings toward you or toward themselves. They must know that *they* are never bad, personally, but that their choices certainly can be.

7. Never assume ownership of your children's behavior.
If you follow this one little rule, you'll find it much easier to keep your cool. And as I've mentioned before, you'll send them the message that you have faith in them to solve their problems on their own or deal with the repercussions if they don't.

8. Minimize the parenting blabber.
The more you plead, lecture, explain, warn, coax, advise, threaten, demand, insist, beg, and negotiate, the more static your children have to cut through to think at all, much less think about their choices. The less you inundate them with words, the less likely they are to become parent-deaf or annoyed.

9. Try to use more positives than negatives.
Words like *no*, *don't*, *quit*, *can't*, and *stop* encourage us to define our children in terms of what they're doing

wrong rather than what they're doing right. They also frustrate our children, because no one wants to be told what they *can't* do all the time. If we use a lot of these words, sooner or later we'll be at almost constant odds with our children. Later on in this section we'll discuss ways to avoid them.

10. Never purposely ignore your children's misbehavior.
This annoys them to the point that they become engrossed in masterminding a counterattack instead of reflecting on their behavior. Besides, how easy is it to ignore the high-decibel screeching that only children can master?

11. Avoid using external influences to get your children to behave.
Resorting to bribes, rewards, threats, ultimatums, and higher authorities like Santa teaches children to look for external guidance. They then learn to base their choices on whether they're going to get caught or not.

12. Never rescue children from the consequences of misbehavior.
When you bail them out by giving them second chances or by not disciplining them in the first place, the behavior you're trying to change is never extinguished. Plus, they don't learn to cope with difficult consequences in the real world. If you use one or more of the following seven techniques for empowering discipline for every incidence of misbehavior and every broken rule, your kids won't be left wondering if this is the time to behave or not. And

again, it gives you yet another opportunity to show them that you have confidence in them to endure hardship.

Seven techniques to bring out your child's heroism

OK, I know some of you are thinking, "Wait just a darn minute! You just took away my best ammo. Now what am I supposed to do, unleash them on the unsuspecting public and hope for the best?" Read on. What follows are seven highly effective discipline techniques that help you implement, in action, the spirit of the twelve tenets of empowering discipline discussed above. Each technique emphasizes your role as mentor and speaks to your children's inner hero by encouraging them to analyze the choices they make.

1. Logical and natural consequences

Consequences that make sense for misbehavior are the meat and potatoes of a discipline program designed to inspire heroism. Remember, heroes consistently make clear and responsible choices based on their own sense of right and wrong rather than on factors beyond their control. When children understand the connection between their actions and the results they produce—both for themselves and others—they will use that knowledge to control their behavior on a conscious rather than a reactive level. This conscious control allows them to steer their behavioral choices using their own values and principles. Only when they can take control of their own choices consistently can they become true everyday heroes.

Two kinds of consequences inspire heroism: logical and natural. Logical consequences differ from natural ones in that they require our subtle intervention. Here's an example. When one of my sons was younger, he had frequent tantrums that made him look like a cross between a whirling dervish and a Tasmanian devil. They seemed to last an eternity, which, given the turmoil they caused within our household, was insufferable. Punishment by iron maiden and thumbscrews seemed a picnic in comparison. None of my tried-and-true techniques appeared to make a dent. One day, he launched into a humdinger just as we were all about to go to the ice cream store. If I remember correctly, it was provoked by some earth-shattering crisis like the seam in his sock wasn't lined up perfectly or one of his siblings was—God forbid—"looking at him."

In the past, I would have threatened to leave him behind, knowing full well I wouldn't follow through. After all, tempting as it was, I couldn't leave a three-year-old at home all alone. Anyway, I felt sorry for him—poor underprivileged child missing out on his favorite ice cream treat: double chocolate fudge covered with gummy bears!

But it soon occurred to me that letting him off the hook was like flicking gasoline on a smoldering fire instead of taking a hose to it. So that day, I calmly told him, "I'm sorry I can't take you with us to the ice cream store, because the other customers want to enjoy their ice cream in peace. But don't worry, I've spoken to Mrs. Vazquez next door, and she's willing to take care of you until we get back."

The tears, promises, begging, and pleading made it tough, but I reminded myself that this was a valuable lesson for my son. I walked him across the street and left him with my neighbor—whom I still owe considerably. When we picked him up afterwards, he seemed different, somehow. He wasn't angry or sulky. He was calm and happy. I truly believe he wanted help controlling his temper and was subconsciously grateful for the limits I enforced. I also think he felt proud that he could weather that storm with flying colors.

A natural consequence is different, because it doesn't require us to interfere. For instance, almost every day, my daughter would forget to bring her lunch to school. Of course, I wanted to show her that it's OK to make a mistake and that we help each other out in such cases, but after the third day, it was time for me to stop waltzing into the school cafeteria with a Happy Meal. After the second incidence, I explained that I had faith in her to come up with ways to remember her lunch and that next time she'd be on her own. Sure enough, on the third day, she called to ask me to bring her a lunch. Not only did I refuse, but I called the school office to make sure they didn't bail her out by loaning her lunch money. I wanted her to learn to resolve her problem on her own, and the natural consequence of a few hours of hunger was a valuable lesson that helped her do so.

Why do natural and logical consequences empower children to find their inner hero? By teaching them that they alone are responsible for the consequences of their actions. Since these consequences make sense in the context of their misbehavior, children don't feel like they're being punished, so they have no one to blame for their poor choice but themselves. They perceive these consequences as something *they* bring on *themselves*. Consequences have an inevitable nature; once a consequence is set in motion, children have no power to stop it. All they can do is brace themselves as the great big tsunami rolls slowly toward them. And as it sweeps our children off their feet, we're tanning in our beach chairs at a safe distance, saying, "Gosh, Honey, I wish there was something I could do, but these are the rules. I can't do anything to change them." As harsh as this may sound, there's no better time than childhood for kids to figure out the connection between choices and consequences. After childhood, the prices of those consequences will no longer be marked down.

2. Limited choices

A hero without choices is like a captain without a ship. A child must be entrusted with choices if he's to become empowered as a lifelong decision-maker. Giving your child choices not only tells him that you have faith in his ability to make decisions on his own, it also provides him with the practice he needs. Limited choices are particularly useful as a discipline tool because they defuse potential conflict. Many a power struggle can be averted by allowing a child to have a part of the power he seeks. Let's look at the three types of limited choices used as a discipline strategy that will wake up your child's inner hero:

> *If/then:* "If you get dressed in time, then you'll have more time to watch cartoons before the bus comes."

> *When/then:* "When you finish your tantrum, then we can go to the park as we planned."

> *This or that:* "It's bedtime. What do you want to do first—take a bath or read a story?"

Two important caveats: First, never use limited choices as bribes or threats, because then the choice becomes an external beacon rather than an intrinsic motive for thinking things through. Second, make sure you're willing to accept the option your child decides on; otherwise, he's just playing a guessing game where he must figure out what it is you really want.

3. Impartial observations

Since everyday heroes control their behavior on a conscious level, our goal as parents is to use discipline that gets our children to think about the pros, cons, alternatives, and consequences for their actions.

By using impartial observations, we can stimulate a child to reflect on her actions before or after they occur. This reflection can help her think clearly before she chooses so she can resist the urge to misbehave or find the motivation to make a positive choice. After the fact, impartial observations can help her examine the consequences for the irresponsible choice in question. This empowers her to recognize, eliminate, and replace poor behavioral patterns.

Impartial observations are a great way to jump-start your child's thinking engines without provoking a defensive or retaliative action. "It's already six o'clock and you haven't started your homework yet" will get a child to reflect on his procrastination and come up with a solution, while "I'm so sick and tired of having to remind you to do your homework—march to your room right now and do it" only makes him feel angry or ashamed.

4. Objective information

Providing children with objective information is another technique that motivates them to analyze their behavior, decide if any changes are needed, and implement those changes consistently. To become heroes at the helm of their own ship, children must have the necessary GPS coordinates to get to their destination without being shipwrecked en route. Sometimes all they need is a bit of information—a way point to help them proceed on course and navigate wisely. Providing objective information gives them that way point so they can analyze a choice internally. It's also a friendly way to remind them about the rules without appearing judgmental. Here are some examples:

> "It's not safe to play with matches," instead of, "Whaddya, nuts? You're gonna burn us all up with those. Off to your room, Mister, and stay there until I say!"

> "Feet do not belong on the table," instead of, "How many times have I told you not to put your filthy feet on my table?"

Using objective information is also a powerful technique for building your family identity and reinforcing your family rules and values:

> "Our family uses words, not hitting," instead of, "Stop hitting your sister!"

> "Our family values the truth," instead of, "You're a liar."

5. "I" messages
Sometimes finger-pointing incites defensive posturing or retaliation in children. Because it's impossible for them to analyze their choices objectively while simultaneously defending their pride or launching a counterattack, any discipline that smacks of accusation detracts them from

focusing on, examining, and modifying their behavior. In other words, our heroes-to-be lose rudder control and are blown off-course. Stomping off to their rooms, slamming their doors, and cranking heavy-metal tunes to wall-rattling levels are a sure indication that they're charting an aimless course toward a hull-ripping reef.

One way to avoid an accusatory air is to use "I" instead of "you." When you voice your feelings in an objective statement instead of a passionate shout every time you are upset, you get your message across without casting blame or provoking a defensive response. For instance, you might say, "I feel upset when you track mud on the floor I just mopped," instead of, "How could you! Do you know how hard I worked to clean that floor?" (By substituting *people* in place of *you* in the first remark, it becomes even less confrontational while still allowing you to express your feelings.)

6. Questioning

Mentoring children to call on their inner hero means asking them to think. After all, how can they recognize and control those forces that try to influence their choices if they use their noggins for little more than hat racks? Help your child seize the opportunity to exercise her thinking muscles by asking open-ended questions. By guiding her through a thought process with a series of questions, you show her what she could be asking herself in the form of internal dialogue. Think of it as training wheels for the brain. Once a child can steer her thoughts without toppling over, she'll be able to take the helm with all the confidence you'd expect in an everyday hero. Here's an example:

"What is our rule about playing the stereo so loudly?" (The child answers.) "Why do we have that rule?" (The child answers.) "What do you need to do now?" (The child answers.)

Compare that to a confrontational threat:

"Knock it off, Johnny! You're gonna make us all deaf! If you don't turn that music down, I'm taking that stereo and tossing it out the window."

7. The minimalist parenting approach

Have you ever had your child come up to you and start chattering while you're busy at the computer or reading? Or how about the incessant "Mom, Mom, Mom, Mom, Mom, Mom, Mom, Mom, Mom, Mom, Mom, Mom!" that kids like to torture us with? Until we reach our breaking point, many of us will let all of that child blabber go in one ear and out the other, dutifully nodding our heads as if we're captivated by every syllable. Well, our children are no different. The more we yak, the less they hear. They become "parent-deaf." And when they can't register what comes out of our mouth, we are ineffective as mentors. To raise a hero, we need to guide our children in a language they can understand—or at least tolerate.

Minimalist parenting is a wonderful way to avoid parental blabber. Use one- to three-word phrases, facial expressions, and gestures. When Johnny drops his jacket on the kitchen floor, point to it and say, "Johnny, jacket!" When Cheryl is talking on the phone past her bedtime, sweep your index finger across your neck—the universal "cut off" sign.

These seven discipline techniques, when delivered politely, respectfully, and calmly, can replace any of the accusatory or judgmental strategies that have been ingrained in our parenting for centuries. And since our children don't usually interpret these techniques as personal attacks, they won't be compelled to retaliate against us or feel bad about themselves. Instead, they're more likely to feel comfortable reflecting on our words and using them to help guide their present and future choices.

These strategies are therefore highly effective in producing desirable behaviors and extinguishing undesirable ones. More important, they encourage our children to make responsible choices because it is the right course of action to take. This is how true heroes make decisions in life.

Setting the example

As our children's mentors, we have a responsibility to model the behavior and qualities we want to instill. Imagine the short-circuiting in our kids' brains if we try to guide them in one direction while we go in the opposite one. This double standard would make it impossible for our children to agree with and abide by our rules and boundaries without finding excuses for breaking them. Furthermore, a good example is important because the more our children respect and admire us, the more power we have to guide them in the direction we want them to go—toward heroism.

I know it may not seem easy to break all the bad habits we've collected over our lives. In fact, because most of us were raised to be externally directed, we might not be able to kick them all. But knowing that parents today want to do the best they can for their children, I don't think there's anybody better suited to take on that challenge.

Modeling empowerment

For children to become independent, self-confident, and comfortable using their inner compass to navigate in a world teeming with unfiltered influences, we need to model self-reliance instead of neediness in our behavior and attitude.

In the past, I used to punt those manly, physical tasks to my husband, because I wasn't sure I could do them successfully. And because of his willingness to help, I really didn't have to confirm or deny my suspicions. But now, in order to model empowerment for my kids, I try to do some of those things myself.

One day, I put up a homemade zip line between two trees in the backyard for my kids to enjoy—and wear themselves out for the day. I made it from gadgets whose names I couldn't pronounce and thingamajiggies I never knew existed: braided steel wire, pulleys, turnbuckles, aluminum ferrules, bolts, pipes, insulating foam (to pad the pipe handles), and other odds and ends. Of course I put the pulleys on upside down and had to cut the wires and start all over—twice—but I was proud of the end result, and the kids have had hours of fun ever since. So that my experience wouldn't go unnoticed, I made sure to voice my accomplishments, setbacks and all, so that my children could understand the satisfaction of meeting a challenge alone.

Modeling empowerment also requires us to resist making less-obvious pleas for rescue, such as manipulation, whether vengeful or coy. There are all sorts of under-handed ways to get others to come to our aid, like sulking, playing the martyr, using threats or ultimatums, or playing the damsel in distress. But these are not hero-building skills; they are devices used by those who can't recognize their own inner heroism—those who lack the confidence to accomplish something alone or to openly and honestly lead others to pitch in.

Modeling sound decision-making skills

If we want our children to feel at ease developing and relying on their own reasoning skills, we need to model the benefits of doing so. When faced with a problem, try to think aloud in front of your child so she can observe the reasoning process you go through to get to a solution.

For instance, say you've piled the kids in the car on Monday morning to drive them to school—only to hear that horrible *whirr-raoww-raoww-raoww* sound when you turn the key in the ignition.

You think aloud, "I know that's not the agonal breaths of a constipated goose. Last time I checked, our yard was free from fowl. Hmmm. (*Your heart sinks to your kneecaps.*) The battery must be dead."

Though your kids are probably whispering, "Yes! No school!" and slapping high fives in the backseat, you go on to solve the problem out loud, much to their dismay: "I can run over to Francine's and borrow her jumper cables, but no, then she's going to have to drive her car up to my garage, and I know how much she hates being seen in her robe with those pink rollers in her hair. Anyway, she'd have to park behind me, and I'm not sure those cables could stretch that far. Tell ya what, I'll ask Kathy to take you guys to school. Then maybe she'll drive me to AutoZone so I can pick up a new battery. Everybody hustle! Let's go ask Ms. Vazquez if she can help us out here. After I drop you guys off, I'll call the school to tell them you'll be five minutes late."

Imagine the joy on your children's angelic little faces. Yeah, right!

You can also think out loud when the problem involves a conflict with another person: "I hope I didn't hurt Aunt Sally's feelings by turning down her offer to play bridge tomorrow. I'll remind her that I've never played before and would make a terrible partner. And I'll take some finger sandwiches over to her so that she and her bridge buddies will have something to nibble on."

It's also helpful to discuss with your children problems that you have already solved successfully by sharing the steps you took in finding solutions: "I remember when I was a kid, I snuck into your Aunt Laura's room for nightly raids on her Easter basket. I loved those little chocolate-covered marshmallow bunnies, and mine were history within minutes. When she found out, she was so mad she wouldn't speak to me for weeks. I felt really bad, because we were very close. So I went from door to door in the neighborhood to raise money walking dogs, sweeping driveways, you name it. When I had enough of a stash, I walked to the 7-11 and bought her a whole box of those bunnies. I wrapped it up in brown paper, tied a home-made bow around it, and hid it under her pillow along with a note saying how sorry I was and how she was the best sister in the whole wide world. It worked like a charm. We were pals again and I felt a lot better. She still kept her basket under lock and key, but it was a good start."

Another way you can model confidence in the power of reason is to show your children that you trust your own intuition. Express any intuitive feelings you have in front of them rather than dismissing them as foolish thoughts: "I don't think we should go to the baseball game this Friday. I have a bad feeling about it. Why don't we go to next week's game instead?" And if those feelings prove to have been well-founded, make sure to share that with them as well. "I'm so glad I trusted my instincts and changed our tickets to next week. Look outside at that weather! That hail would have made dents in our car the size of Wyoming!"

Because inner honesty is essential for our children if they are to develop and rely on their own compass, model integrity for your children. Try not to excuse your wrong-doings, justify your mistakes, or blame others for poor choices. If you catch yourself in the act, verbalize that out loud: "What am I talking about? I can't make excuses for snapping at the checkout clerk like that. After all, it wasn't her fault that the computers went down, making her re-scan all three carts full of my groceries. I'm going to turn back and apologize. It's the least I can do."

By rebounding from our failures, we show our children that we have faith in our decision-making abilities even when we fail. If they get wind of the fact that our failures have shaken our confidence in ourselves, they might lose faith in their own decision-making when failure rears its ugly head.

When appropriate, make a point to share your failures, and discuss the benefits you have reaped from them. For instance, a couple of years ago, I decided to replace our Persian rugs. The decision was difficult because, being handwoven from the finest wool, they were pretty expensive. But they were also at least eighteen years old. And thanks to a legacy of housebreaking puppies, they emitted that *eau de pee* smell that nothing short of Clorox or Drano would remove. In other words, those rugs were attracting more flies than compliments.

Boy, was I proud when I stumbled on a line of rugs that looked almost exactly like our old ones—minus the decorative yellow spots—for a fraction of the price! With a cocky air that translated to "I am the Queen of Budgetdom," I laid down those new carpets and tossed the others in the trash.

To anyone with a functioning set of eardrums, I'd announce, "They're a polyester-wool mix, but don't they look great?" And yep, they did look great just long enough for me to parade my neighbors in front of them and turn them on to the deal of a lifetime. With the exception of my milkman and the grocery sacker, they all bought a set for their own homes.

But a few weeks later, after fourteen human feet—give or take a few—and twelve paws had trampled mercilessly over them, the ends were unraveling and the designs were wearing down to the nubs. It was almost enough to drive me to the city landfill to reclaim my old rugs. Nevertheless, I told my children that disaster and opportunity are opposite sides of the same coin. From that disaster, I seized the opportunity to learn a lesson that probably saved me a lot of money and aggravation in the future: You get what you pay for.

My kids have learned that my stumbles, defeats, and mistakes are not signs that I'm incompetent—they're experiences that have brought me one step closer to achieving my goals, realizing my dreams, and unleashing my own inner heroism. If you model your own decision-making techniques and give your kids a living example of integrity, when it comes time for them to make their own mistakes, your example will be the shining path leading them on to heroic decisions.

Modeling strong character

Everyday heroes don't flinch in the face of temptations and urges. They don't shirk what's right because it's inconvenient or difficult. And they certainly don't do what's wrong because they think they can get away with it—they show strength of character. Having a strong character goes beyond adhering to a skeletal framework of values—it means taking all our principles and values into account with every decision we make, whether small or large, easy or tough. It means considering other's feelings before we make a choice. It means being willing to sacrifice for a greater good. To raise our children as heroes, we must model this strength of character in our own attitudes and behavior. These qualities include

- *A high sense of accountability and responsibility.* You can demonstrate your healthy work ethic by resisting the urge to call in sick when you're scheduled to work during a school holiday. You can honor your commitment to chaperone at the middle-school dance even though your bunions are on a rampage. You can 'fess up when you eat the last brownie instead of blaming it on Fido.
- *Loyalty and respect toward friends, family, and other key people in our lives.* You can stick up for

friends, family, or even acquaintances who are the butt of gossip that is either unfair, untrue, or both. You can show good manners even to those who treat you rudely. You can help shoulder the duties and responsibilities of those in your life when they are unable to do so because of illness or other circumstances.

- *Compassion, tolerance, and empathy.* Everyone wants to be unconditionally loved and accepted. Even those who aren't thin or don't have flawless skin. Even those who oppose your religious or political views. Even those who have hurt you. Being kind and understanding to everyone in your life only requires you to accept them for who they are. You don't have to accept their poor choices or agree with them on all points. For instance, because my family is so large, when I order popcorn and drinks at the concession stand, it tries the patience of anyone standing behind me. One day a grumpy old man started to fume, heave sighs of annoyance, and mutter remarks under his breath not fit for my children's G-rated hearing. Finally he said something nasty out loud, inspiring a collective gasp from the line of people behind him. I simply turned around and gazed at him for a while, trying hard to see him through compassionate eyes. No easy task juggling five popcorns, two boxes of Milk Duds, and seven soft drinks, with two children pulling on my skirt pleading frantically for me to take them to the restroom. Then I said in the kindest voice I could muster, "I'm so sorry you've had to wait so long. I know it must be very difficult to follow an order like mine, wondering if you're going to miss the first part of your movie. Please accept my apology. And to show my appreciation for your patience, allow me to pay for your refreshments this evening." At first, the old man was speechless. After all, he was expecting a scathing reply or a slap, not kindness and generosity. As it turned out, he apologized for his remark, refused my offer to pay, and since we were going to the same movie, he actually joined us and provided excellent company. All that and we still made it to the restroom on time.

- *Sacrifice.* When you get called for jury duty, you can sacrifice the luncheon you planned with your friends for another time. If your neighbor asks you to watch her toddler while she takes her sick cat to the vet, you can sacrifice the television show you've been waiting a week to watch.

- *Self-discipline and perseverance.* You can resist the urge to cast your exercise program to the winds because "Exercising is futile in the face of my big-boned and zaftig genetic legacy." You can keep on trying to sew your own summer cocktail dress even when it starts to look more like a cross between an oversized muumuu and your grandmother's kitchen drapes.

- *Not showing an unreasonable sense of entitlement or expecting reciprocity for your good deeds.* For instance, when your friend doesn't utter one word of thanks when you help him move in, you can still tell your children how good it made you feel to lend a helping hand. When your boss neglects to give you the Christmas bonus you've staked your budget on year after year, you can revise that budget and comment on the difficult times the company is going through, how lucky you are to have a job, and ways you can help turn the red ink into black.

In short, a strong character is all about courage—the courage to resist the easy way out; to ignore our selfish desires; to tolerate our own suffering or discomfort; to take on conflicts, challenges, and other difficulties when it is the right thing to do.

Modeling self-direction

Because of the externally directed upbringing most of us had and because we live in a culture that sets unrealistic standards, it's difficult even for us adults to swim upstream against the forceful current of media and pop-culture messages. But if we want our children to be heroes, we need to give them the tools and the power to consciously filter these messages, choosing to accept those that will benefit them and reject those that won't.

We need to set a proper example of independent thinking by putting our own external direction aside as much as possible. Here are some suggestions:

- Resist following the latest trends in music, consumer goods, hairstyles, and fashions unless you truly like them. If you do follow a fad or standard, make sure your children understand your reasoning. For example, if you just bought the latest in tennis shoes, you might say, "I like the way these shoes look with my shorts, and they feel so comfortable on my feet. I don't really care what other people think about them. One look at my T-shirt riddled with holes and covered with baby-burp stains ought to make that pretty obvious!"

- Resist feeling pressured to comply with physical or lifestyle standards that you dislike, that are unattainable, or that don't fit your budget. We get a zit once in a while. We put on a few pounds. We have bad hair days six days a week. We don't have a second home. So what? Does that mean we have to schedule emergency consults with the dermatologist, plastic surgeon, hairstylist, and realtor? Model contentment with your own situation; show your kids by your example that it's OK to be just the way we are rather than how others expect us to be. (I feel better already!)

- Try not to support media that deliver conformist propaganda, and boycott programming, magazines, products, and other blameworthy sources. For instance, when I see those commercials that show gorgeous women relaxing on twenty-million-dollar yachts smoothing French suntan lotion on the flawless, bronzed skin covering their Cindy Crawford-esque bodies, I get this strong urge to get into my car, drive to the nearest Walgreen's, and buy a case of generic suntan lotion to keep my own less-than-perfect body from crisping like a slice of bacon in hot grease. Simple bottles. No advertisements. Low cost. Not only am I spared the dilemma of choosing between cutting my grocery bill and putting braces on my daughter's buckteeth, but I don't have to be the sucker who buys in to ridiculous claims or endorses the unrealistic ideals the media often sets for us. I go a step beyond modeling media-independent thought by sharing my ideas with my children. While watching an actress transform her tresses from what looks like a tangle of earthworms shriveled on hot asphalt to silky locks so shiny that you have to wear sunglasses to look at them, I might ask them, "If I use that shampoo, do you think my hair will look like hers?" Naturally they laugh to the point of tears and asphyxia. Nonetheless, I go on: "Why do you think the advertisers of that product lead me to believe I can? Do you think I should support companies that make promises they can't keep? If not, what are my alternatives?" Together, we can come up with several options: buying natural, organic shampoos that don't make such claims; buying generic, no-brand substitutes; buying products made by a small company or produced locally; or shaving my head bald and running my wig through the wash once a week. It's also important to point out hidden bias, like when a morning show praises a movie produced by its parent organization.

- Let your kids know that you march to the beat of your *own* drum—that you refuse to buy in to things that you wouldn't otherwise choose for yourself. Make it a family virtue by saying, "All the girls seem to be wearing that new style of jacket they're selling at The Gap. I don't find them very attractive, plus they cost an arm and a leg. But we Sawyers don't buy into fads unless we really like them. No sirree, we're freethinkers, not sheep who don't have a mind of their own."

- Some people make a sport out of mocking others. In fact, why it's not an Olympic event by now is beyond me. I can see it now, Olympians lined up in their La-Z-Boys, beer in one hand, remote in the other, ready to spew forth a rapid succession of scathing insults. Do your best to refrain from criticizing others for how they look, how they talk, how they act, or what they wear, whether that person is someone you know, a stranger in public, or someone on television or in the movies. When children hear you mocking people, they not only develop a negative attitude toward others and get the message that it's OK to be cruel, they may believe that unless they conform to set standards and trends, they, too, will be subject to criticism or ridicule. Plus, this all adds to the winner/loser mentality that is so sadly prevalent in our culture today.

Even though I'm still externally directed to a certain degree, trying to model these things for my kids has given me the courage to define my own standards and ideals instead of blindly following the crowd. It's amazing how loving our children deeply can inspire us to become better people! Children truly are our greatest teachers.

Surrounding yourself with support

We're embarking on an important mission, you and I—the mission to unlock the true potential in our heroes-to-be. To support your efforts, it's important to find and bring allies into your life—people who share similar attitudes regarding children and parenting. Although we'll go into greater detail on developing and nurturing alliances, you can start by using every opportunity to discuss the issues in this book with educators, other parents, and anyone else with a vested interest in young people and society's future.

I talk to as many folks as I can about the rescue phenomenon, the importance of believing in children and in guiding them to become everyday heroes, successes I've had following the suggestions in this book, and how my parenting approach has affected my own life, my children's lives, and the overall well-being of my family.

I've taken my soapbox beyond the usual audience by talking to strangers on park benches, sackers helping me take my two tons of groceries to the car, and the shampoo lady at the beauty salon. Heck, even my dogs aren't safe around me.

One effective way of creating alliances is to organize a neighborhood parenting network that meets regularly, either at school or in someone's home. Meetings could be devoted to discussing school-related issues, ways to form other alliances, trends among children and adolescents in the neighborhood, as well as child-rearing challenges and other parenting issues. You might even arrange for community leaders and experts in parenting or child development to be guest speakers. Other potential allies in your mission are law-enforcement agencies, churches and synagogues, schools, and anyone else who directly impacts children. Like you, their goal is to inspire integrity within the community, child by child.

In building a network of support, take care to nurture these bonds so that they remain constructive rather than adversarial. For instance, many parents develop contentious relationships with their children's teachers rather than fostering a parent/teacher bond that has the child's best interests at heart.

When you actively seek it, you will find the community rich with treasures of support. So many people and organizations are willing and eager to pull together where children are concerned, especially when the common goal is recognizing and bringing out the inner hero within them.

8

Creating a Family Identity
That Inspires Heroism

The family is the nucleus of civilization.

—William James Durant

Now that we've reexamined our roles as parents and better understand the adjustments we need to make in our behavior and attitude, let's take a look at how the family fits into the grand scheme of things. How can the family, as a unit, help encourage heroism in its children?

The answer: by establishing a strong sense of solidarity. Without common goals, well-defined values, constructive traditions and rituals, and meaningful roles for each of its members, families have identities that are so weak they're often blown off-course. In his book *The Seven Habits of Highly Effective Families*, Stephen R. Covey claims that all strong families have three things in common:

1. *A clear vision of their destination.* Collectively and individually, the family has values, priorities, and goals that are well-defined.

2. *A flight plan that will take them to that destination.* Certain principles that are universal, timeless, and self-evident represent the framework of a flight plan which can help any family move together in a positive direction. Let's take respect as an example. When family members treat each other with respect by solving their differences constructively through compromise and negotiation rather than insults and aggression and by listening with an empathetic ear rather than ignoring or criticizing, they grow stronger by leaps and bounds, both together and individually.

3. *A compass that will guide them through turbulence.* The principles within the family flight plan can be applied to any situation that could throw

the family off-course: tragedies, overwhelming changes, unforeseeable events, and so on.

These three qualities aren't ingrained in some lucky families' collective DNA. They are within any family's reach. But you can't win them in a sweepstakes, rub a magic lamp to get them, or order them online. It takes a conscious effort to construct them.

Once you establish a strong family identity, you transform yourself from a "me" to a "we" mentality. Your children become an important part of the whole—an indispensable piece of the family puzzle. And this united sense of direction, purpose, and belonging is essential to the emerging hero.

Children who develop a hero's inner strength and wisdom generally come from families with a strong sense of unity forged by clear, constructive principles and who respect the differences and appreciate the strengths of individual members. Children from families with weak identities have no steady compass and therefore no clear direction to follow. They often seek guidance from outside sources to gain the sense of unity, purpose, and belonging they lack. Sometimes those sources have their best interests at heart; sometimes they don't.

To establish and strengthen your own family's unique identity, make a conscious, collective effort to

- Show and encourage a respect for rules, and teach your children the reason for and importance of each one. For instance, the car stays put until all seatbelts are on rather than frantically fumbling to snap them shut only when a patrol car appears in the rearview mirror. Children must understand that safety belts are designed to save our lives, not our police records. Establishing and enforcing a clear set of rules and boundaries for each member strengthens family unity. Predictable guidelines for behavior and responsibilities are essential to greasing the gears in the family machinery, allowing it to operate smoothly and efficiently. When your children are mature enough, they can share in the decision-making involved in establishing and changing these rules.

- Show and encourage respect for others, both within and outside the family. This includes demonstrating good manners and gratitude as well as showing respect to your own children, as we will discuss later on.
- Show and encourage compassion, tolerance, and understanding for others, both within and outside the family. Sometimes I challenge my children to conduct experiments in kindness. For instance, when they have a bitter disagreement with a sibling, I all but double-dare one to say something to the other like, "I'm sorry we're not getting along. If there's anything I can do to make things right, let me know," and then calmly walk away without expecting a response. Nine times out of ten, the other sibling will respond with a hug, an apology, or in the case of the male species, a macho comment like, "Hey, we cool or what?" Opportunities abound to share the message that kindness is a powerful instrument in any relationship.
- Show and encourage honesty, loyalty, responsibility, and other qualities congruent with integrity.

A strong family identity united by specific beliefs makes it easier to instill these values in your children.

For instance, when one of my children tries to back out of a baby-sitting commitment, I might say, "The Medhus family believes in keeping their promises."

If one tells a lie, I'll say, "The Medhus family honors the truth."

If one abuses a friendship, I might say, "The Medhus family believes in being loyal to their friends."

Statements like these also have the advantage of being non-accusatory and are therefore less likely to elicit an angry or resentful reaction. (There are rare exceptions. After one of these remarks, my youngest announced she would no longer be a part of the Medhus family. At this writing, she has not, however, packed her bags or purchased her bus ticket.)

Seven steps toward a strong family

What specific actions can you take to create a family identity? Here are some ideas:

1. Establish a hierarchy of priorities that reflect your values and beliefs. For instance, if your son has an important soccer game coming up, clear your work schedule to attend and root him on. If your daughter seems "down in the dumps," cancel your manicure and take her out for a "Buddy Day." After all, family members are always there for each other in times of need and for plain old-fashioned companionship.
2. Nurture relationships within your family, and make sure each family member commits to cultivating

these bonds over time. The most crucial factor for success here is to avoid passing judgment on one another and to offer a generous supply of unconditional love and acceptance.

3. Encourage each family member to think independently. Support your child's attempts to resist conformity, peer pressure, or the lure of mass media and pop culture. Siblings are particularly powerful here. Our family cherishes the motto "Dare to be yourself," so I often overhear one of my children saying something to another like, "Who cares what everyone else thinks. You should wear your hair in whatever style you want!" Similarly, family members should encourage independent, age-appropriate behavior in one another. When your youngest struggles to pour Froot Loops into his cereal bowl, encourage the others to cheer him on with words of support rather than of doubt or ridicule. When your teenager is tormented over whether to ask his crush to the prom, encourage his siblings to build his confidence by saying something like, "Are you kidding man? She'd be lucky to have you as her date!" instead of "I'd hate to be in your shoes. What if she laughs in your face?"

4. Lead your family in advocating a particular cause or performing a service as a united front. You could call a meeting to discuss the contribution you all wish to make, how you will accomplish it, and when you wish to do so. Everybody's input should be considered equally and with respect. Although some families engage in ongoing service projects that require weekly if not daily involvement, even

annual service projects will give your family a strong sense of purpose. Our family likes to do something special around Christmas like passing out jackets, socks, mittens, and blankets to homeless people, singing carols in a nearby nursing home, or dressing up as Santa's elves and delivering small toys to the patients in the pediatric wing of the local hospital. If you have time and ambition for more frequent service to the community, your family can devote two hours per week performing activities where even the youngest can pitch in: picking up litter in the neighborhood park, shoveling snow from sidewalks and driveways of the elderly or disabled, volunteering at a shelter, and so on. Later in the book, I'll provide several resources for service programs that welcome families who enjoy volunteering together.

5. Establish the family as a haven where each member can feel safe and loved. There are several ways to do this. First, help each person feel good about his or her place within the family. By providing opportunities to contribute something meaningful to the group and by making sure he or she feels accepted and loved, each family member gains a strong sense of belonging. Rather than feeling like a superfluous appendage, they know they are the vital organs that keep the family alive and healthy. For instance, during dinner our family often shares what we feel are each member's unique role and the adverse effect that would occur if his or her contributions weren't made. Second, help each family member to feel good about themselves as individuals. At

dinner, ask each person to point out the unique differences of each family member, including their interests, talents, personality, ideas, and opinions. As a family, encourage each other to show appreciation for these differences and take them seriously. Let these family discussions be non-threatening environments where each member feels free to voice ideas, concerns, and opinions without fear of ridicule, objections, or criticism.

6. Another way to help family members feel good about themselves is to establish a healthy attitude regarding mistakes and failures. Not only should family members allow for each other's mistakes and failures, they should encourage them as requirements for personal growth. Try having "mistake contests" where every person describes the biggest blunders they made that day and the lessons learned from them. Another way to help children feel comfortable with their mistakes is to freely admit your own and let them see you apologize.

7. Traditions and routines strengthen a family's identity. Special meals, holidays, or sayings; a yearly vacation destination; a silly way of singing "Happy Birthday"; father-daughter outings; mother-son outings; weekly activities as a group, such as watching old family videos every Sunday, are all examples. Some traditions serve as powerful tools for instilling values such as appreciation and gratitude in children. For example, every Thursday evening, our family gets together to write an anonymous letter of gratitude to a teacher, the police depart-

ment, a friend, or anyone else who contributes something special to our lives.

By establishing a strong family identity, you build a ship whose stability keeps it afloat in the most tumultuous winds and roughest seas. Its solid hull is impenetrable to the rocks and reefs you may sail across as a family. Nestled in such security, children feel comfortable with who they are, where they belong, how they can contribute, and who they can become. When children have this clear sense of self, they develop confidence in their ability to make responsible choices on their own—choices only a hero can make.

9

Building a Mentoring Relationship with Our Children

Teaching is lighting the lamp and not filling the bucket.

—Frank Crane

Once we've made the necessary changes in our role as parents and redefined and strengthened our family's identity, the groundwork crucial to establishing a healthy mentoring relationship with our children has been laid.

As our children's mentors, our job is to help them build a strong sense of self—on their terms, not ours—and to encourage them to express and celebrate their uniqueness. Sometimes mentoring requires us to address our children's behavior immediately and directly, while other times we'll need to watch from the sidelines as the consequences of their behavior become their teacher. Either way, this will mean kicking some stubborn habits that have become entrenched in our own behavior.

Every parenting mistake I describe in this book I've made with my own five children—sometimes consistently! I still mess up from time to time, whereupon my children announce, "Mommy, you need to go read your book again!" But it isn't necessary to be perfect. Even when I've batted 50 percent or so, I can see a huge, positive impact on my children, my family, and my own life. Imagine my relief!

You might wonder how my kids are turning out, given my lapses. Naturally there are still days when I feel like shielding them from the public eye, but those days come less and less often. As a general rule, kids raised to be self-directed start off pretty wild, because learning from experience takes more time and patience than having life spoon-fed to them by force or indulgence. Slowly but surely, though, they mature into strong oaks. Kids raised by managers, slaves, or dictators tend to seem more grown up earlier on, but only because of the external forces making them behave that way. These children become willows, not oaks.

My kids are also comfortable in their own skins. They have their own unique personalities, tastes, and opinions, which they express with all the zeal of a newly released POW. Furthermore, they have no problem fending off peer pressure. One is even fondly referred to by her friends as the "moral police" of the group, because she insists they choose wisely. All of them are leaders among their peers, but leaders who inspire rather than control.

Although they still have some miles to go, all five of my "oaks" have the strength it takes to know themselves, be themselves, and make choices based on what they've determined, through experience, observation, and quiet reflection, to be right. All I can say is, "Pity the fool who tries to push or lure them off-course!"

I'm not sure why batting only 50 percent brings such remarkable results, but I have one theory. Encouraging self-direction in children causes them to see all parenting that fails to do so as unacceptable. It's as if they stumble into an absolute truth. Just as they can't fully understand the concept of hot without having experienced cold, or love without hate, after children experience parenting that grooms them into heroes, all other approaches seem flawed. So instead of our occasional child-rearing set-backs provoking resentment or shame, our kids begin to see our mistakes as "something Mommy and Daddy need to work on." Children learn that, like them, we too are works in progress.

Children see this new type of parenting as so superior to our old ways that they respond quickly to our guidance. These strategies are fair, firm, and loving. They prod children to examine, be accountable for, and change their own behavior. Once kids recognize the power they have over their choices, they take command of the steering wheel so that they can quickly dodge the potholes in their path.

I focus a lot on children's feelings, but what about ours? After all, kids are no different from other people; they are potential sources of frustration and anger—some more than others! As you read on, you may ask, "Am I allowed to get angry?" The answer is a resounding "*Yes!*" If you hide your anger or other negative feelings, you're teaching your child that these must be kept under wraps, not aired. Harboring negative feelings rather than using them constructively and then releasing them is like swallowing battery acid—it keeps gnawing away, eroding you from the inside out.

Your anger should serve as a signal to your child that you're not happy with a choice she's making. The key is to express your upset constructively so that your remarks are motivators for positive change instead of weapons of vengeance. Throughout the remainder of this chapter, I will give specific examples on how to do this.

A final word: Although you should always be the primary mentor in your child's life, help her establish healthy relationships with adults outside the family who you believe are good role models. Then allow these mentoring relationships to develop on their own, rather than forcing them. Later, I'll discuss ways to establish these bonds and provide some resources that can help.

Building a strong sense of self

The first goal of a hero-in-training is to establish a strong sense of self. Although kids must define their own identity, sometimes they need guidance, feedback, and encouragement. They also, at times, simply need a nonjudgmental mentor who has the courage to stand by and allow them to fumble along until they find themselves. For teens who are confused about who they are, one of my favorite books is *Life Strategies for Teens* and the accompanying workbook. The author, Jay McGraw, is the college-age son of Dr. Phil McGraw. He does a wonderful job of talking to his fellow teens in a language they can understand and in a context to which they can relate. The workbook stimulates self-reflection and objective self-assessment. If you encourage your teen to read the book and go through the workbook, he'll embark on a journey of self-discovery that some adults have yet to travel.

Allowing for imperfections

The safest environment for kids to explore their sense of self is one without external appraisal. They must learn to assess their own strengths and weaknesses if they're to find out who they truly are. Evaluations from others only tell them what other people want them to be. To encourage a self-directed child, discipline and parent/child communication must be free of subjective judgments.

This appraisal-free parenting requires us to tolerate our children's imperfections. If we try to urge them to perfection with negative or positive judgments, then we are the ones designing their identity. It also requires us to allow for differences in personality. Children aren't always cut from the same mold as their parents. Their personalities need room to emerge, and their tastes need time to be defined through experimentation. Parents who impose their personal preferences on their children risk forcing an identity crisis. This makes for a very confused and unhappy kid. Furthermore, children who have parent-defined identities are usually in for a shock the minute they cross that middle-school threshold. Suddenly this artificially crafted persona leaves them vulnerable to peer criticism and even rejection. So then they have to establish a whole new identity to satisfy their peers.

I've watched one of my daughter's classmates grow up since kindergarten. Through the first half of grade school, her parents always made sure she had on frilly, expensive dresses, her hair was immaculately combed and tied up with ribbons, and her shoes were sparkling. They also placed demanding academic expectations on her. If she made a B on her report card, she was grounded. If she missed a note during her piano recital, she was scolded. As she entered fourth grade, the parents pressured her to fit in. Out with the frilly dresses and hair ribbons and in with Abercrombie and Fitch. If there was a new hairstyle, the mom would cart her off to the stylist. If everyone was going to an "in" summer camp, her daughter simply had to go. If everyone else had boyfriends, her daughter was no loser; so she would have to have one too. The mom hosted a girl/boy dance party in her home when her daughter was in fifth grade. We're talking elementary-school kids, people. Most of them prepubertal. (Gosh, if my husband had his way, my daughters wouldn't be allowed to go to their senior prom! Not unless he was allowed to hover within two inches of them and their dates, stun gun in hand. Heck, he'd pick their dates if he could. Eunuchs—prime candidates.)

What happened to this girl once she entered middle school? She became completely lost. The identity her parents had crafted for her over the years made her a laughingstock. She earned the reputation as a stuck-up, nerdy "prep" who was a prude to boot. (Being a "prude" may be a parent's dream, but it doesn't fly well among newbie adolescents.) She reacted by going to the extreme—piercing her tongue, eyebrows, lips, and God knows what else; experimenting with drugs; engaging in gratuitous sex; dressing in Goth garb. Ten to one she still has no idea who she is.

I think the notorious teen-rebellion phenomenon that drives some of us parents to get our tubes tied or run away from home results from this identity conflict rather than natural biological factors. Sure, hormones add fuel to the fire, but by encouraging our kids to win our approval, we craft them to become the people *we* want them to be rather than the heroes they're destined to be. In the following sections, you'll see some of the tools we parents use to sculpt our kids into our particular vision of a masterpiece. It's no wonder some kids today live double lives—acting like cherubs around adults, only to become Marilyn Mansons around their peers.

Why we judge our children and why we shouldn't

We parents often use judgments—both positive and negative—as electric cattle prods that keep our children on the course we want them to follow. Positive prods tell kids, "You're on the right path to creating an identity that we find acceptable." Negative ones tell them, "Get into chute number five, little doggie! You're not going where *we* want you to go!" Although both may be effective in getting our little calves from the prairie to the processing plant, their true identities wind up getting slaughtered and turned into flank steak. (That's the Texas in me talking.)

Negative evaluations breed resentment and upset family harmony. They can also erode children's self-esteem. Positive evaluations aren't much better. By artificially inflating kids' self-esteem, we set them up for a rude awakening later on. And sometimes when a parent praises a child, the first thing that comes to the child's mind is when she came up short. For instance, if a child hears praise like, "Look how spotless your room is! You are such a tidy person," the first thing she'll think about will probably be the time she got fussed at for living in a pigsty, not what a perfect prodigy she is. We'll examine helpful forms of praise in the "How to Become an Objective Parent" section that follows.

All forms of judgmental parenting hamper a child's ability to assess himself objectively. Without this important skill, he will rely on the opinions others have of him instead of forming his own. To be an everyday hero, our children must be able to evaluate their own strengths, weaknesses, and performance in life.

Here are examples of parental appraisals to avoid:

Negative evaluations
- *Criticism:* "Your hair's a mess."
- *Nagging:* We all know this one. It's when we keep drilling even after we hit oil.
- *Reprimand:* "How dare you treat your little sister that way!"

- *Negative labels:* "You're so clumsy!"
- *Negative comparisons:* "Why can't you be truthful like your brother?"
- *Negative generalizations:* "You *always* forget to hang up your jacket," or "You *never* turn your assignments in on time."
- *Guilt-provoking statements, including martyrdom:* "OK, I'll drive you to school, but if you keep missing the bus and making me late for work, I'm probably going to get fired," or "If you really loved me, you'd stop talking back all the time."
- *Shame-provoking statements:* "How in the world did you not make the tennis team? With all the private lessons you took, you should be able to beat Sampras by now," or "You should know better than to do something like that!"
- *Personal insults and angry remarks:* "You're just no good! I'm sick of putting up with you!"
- *Negative rhetorical questions:* "Why can't you just behave?"

Positive evaluations

- *Judgmental affirmations that address the child rather than the behavior:* "You're such a good boy."
- *Judgmental affirmations that make allowances for the child's problems or weaknesses:* "Don't worry, kiddo. I got picked on a lot at your age too."
- *Positive labels:* "You're the creative genius of the family."
- *Positive comparisons:* "You've got to be the smartest kid in school!"

- *Positive generalizations:* "You're *always* so polite toward adults," or "You *never* break your promises."
- *Other harmful forms of praise:* Generalized praise ("Wow, awesome job!"); excessive, indiscriminant, or insincere praise ("How's my little genius today?"); and praising the accoutrements (trophies and other prizes) of a child's successes rather than the steps she took to get there.

How to become an objective parent

To parent in a nonjudgmental way, use strategies to guide or praise your child that aren't forms of appraisal. Try the techniques from chapter 7: objective information, "I" messages, impartial observations, limited choices, minimalist parenting, questioning, and logical and natural consequences.

Here's how these techniques would work on some of the examples of negative evaluations listed above:

Instead of "OK, I'll drive you to school, but if you keep missing the bus and making me late for work, I'm probably going to get fired," try an impartial observation before your child is hopelessly behind: "I see you haven't eaten your breakfast yet, and the bus comes in five minutes."

Instead of "Why can't you be truthful like your brother?" try providing objective information: "People appreciate being told the truth."

Instead of saying, "You *always* forget to hang up your jacket," try the minimalist approach by saying your child's name and pointing to the jacket.

A logical consequence can replace the remark, "You *never* turn your assignments in on time." For instance, you might team up with your son's teacher to come up with suitable consequences: perhaps he'll be required to finish incompleted assignments during recess, at lunch, or after school. If he leaves completed work at home, the teacher could have him repeat the entire assignment in class. Or if grades are important to him, he can get a zero for every incomplete or forgotten assignment.

A natural consequence would be perfect in the case of the child who keeps missing the bus. Let him walk to school, if it's safe. Or drive her, on your own schedule, which means she'll be late. This works great for kids who hate to draw attention to themselves by walking into class late. Natural consequences would also work for the kid who failed to make the tennis team. His disappointment is consequence enough. In fact, good parenting would focus on the positive aspects of his attempts by praising his internal achievements rather than pointing out the external goal he failed to attain: "I admire the perseverance you showed throughout this," or "I respect the dedication you showed in working so hard to prepare."

Limited choices could be used to replace these judgmental remarks:

In place of "If you really loved me, you'd stop talking back all the time," try saying, "When you feel you can speak respectfully, then we can finish our conversation and work this out together."

Instead of "Your hair's a mess," you could say, "It's almost time to go to the bus stop. What do you want to do first—pack your lunch or brush your hair?"

Questioning can replace "You *never* turn your assignments in on time." It might go something like this, with one question following another, each one forcing the child to think through the situation himself:

"I see you've forgotten to turn in your assignment again. What rule does the school have about that?" (When the child has to voice the rule, he has to understand it clearly.)

"Why do you think they have that rule?" (Now the child must think about and articulate the reasons behind the rule.)

"Why do you think you have trouble remembering this responsibility? (Here, he will try to figure out what he lacks that causes this problem.)

"What do you need to do to help yourself remember?" (With this question, you indicate you have faith that he can solve this problem. Here, he will come up with strategies to help solve this recurring mistake. Offer suggestions, especially if you present them as memory strategies that have helped you in the past.)

It's a good idea to practice appraisal-free parenting by reflecting on instances of judgmental parenting (your own or others) and then mentally substituting one or more of the seven hero-building strategies.

Replace your positive evaluations with more objective approaches so that your child can develop his own inner praise process—a skill that will steel him against negative peer pressure, bullying, teasing, and other attacks to his self-esteem. Try these five alternatives to externally generated praise:

1. *"I" Messages:* "It really helps me out when you watch the baby for an hour or two every day. I feel

confident that she is in good hands, and I can have a nice rest."

2. *Impartial observations:* "I've been noticing how good you're getting at making conversation with adults. Did you see how pleased and surprised Uncle Mike was when you asked him how his garden was doing?" Remarks like these are devoid of personal judgment, so instead of focusing on what needs to be done to remain in our good favor, our children are prompted to reflect on their choices.

3. *Silent praise:* A nod, wink, pat on the back, smile, kiss, hug, or thumbs up. Sometimes the less said, the more genuine the message. Our children are so used to our prattle that they often become "parent-deaf." Just as a whisper will perk up their ears, a gesture will grab their attention.

4. *Overheard praise:* While you know your child is listening, but he isn't aware that you know he's there, sing high praises about his accomplishment to your spouse, another family member, a neighbor, or friend. "Did you see the kicks Adam made during the soccer game? All his hard work at the practices really shows!" When children hear someone praise them in their absence, that praise comes off as more sincere—devoid of ulterior motive. For that reason, it packs a more powerful punch.

5. *Questioning:* Questions guide our children through a self-assessment process while leaving our opinions, criticisms, and unsolicited suggestions out of the picture: "What do you think the best part of your geography project is?" "How did you come up with the idea to shade the borders that way?"

"What was the most difficult part of the project?"
"What did you do to overcome that problem?"
"How did you feel when you finished it?"

Practice replacing your own pet judgmental or ineffective praises with alternatives from these five categories. In all of these objective forms of praise, parents play the role of enthusiastic spectator rather than fairground judge. After all, our children need our positive feedback and encouragement, not our pride or approval, in order to learn how to objectively assess their performance on their own. Once children can praise themselves from within, they can sincerely appreciate their strengths. Heroes must recognize their own potential for greatness in order to move those mountains.

When we eliminate judgments—negative or positive—our children will feel comfortable with the mentor/disciple relationship we're trying to establish. They won't feel the need to defend their pride or self-worth. They won't have the urge to retaliate. They won't immerse themselves in self-deprecating thoughts. They won't look to others to measure their performance.

Without these harmful distractions, our children are free to think for themselves: to find solutions to their problems, to consider the consequences for their mistakes, to determine the soundness of their choices, and to shape their own identities. In short, they'll think like heroes.

Avoiding conditional love and acceptance

When you place conditions on your love, unintentional or not, your child feels like she must work tooth and nail to win your approval. How do we imply that our love or acceptance comes with strings attached? Let me count the ways:

Love qualifiers

"I love you, but I wish you'd be more dependable."

"I love you when you pick flowers for me."

"I'd love you if you'd bring your poor old mom her slippers."

Try to keep your statements of love separate from your feedback and requests. Here are some examples of alternatives to the qualifiers above:

"I get so frustrated when I come home from work to find dinner hasn't been started yet."

"You seem to know exactly when I need a pick-me-up. Things were pretty rough at work, but getting a bouquet of beautiful wildflowers from you makes me feel a hundred percent better."

"Could you bring me my slippers, Honey? I'm tired to the bone and don't think I could muster enough energy to blink, much less fetch anything."

Apology qualifiers

"I'm sorry I spanked you, but you know how I can't stand a lot of racket while I'm reading my paper."

As you can see here, qualifiers tend to negate or lessen the sincerity of our apologies. It's best to separate your apology from your discipline or negative feedback.

In this example, you could say, "I'm sorry I spanked you. I don't believe in laying a hand on my children, and I should have kept myself under control. Please accept my apology."

Later on (not within the next five minutes or so), address your child's misbehavior: "You all were making a lot of noise while I was trying to read my paper. The living room is a place we can go to get peace and quiet. I want you to respect that in the future."

Demands for reciprocity

"The least you can do is thank me for all the help I gave you on your homework last night!"

Instead of demanding gratitude, focus on how good it felt helping someone you love.

Nevertheless, we don't want to raise a pack of thoughtless brats, so we must teach children to express appreciation. There are many ways you can do this. For instance, verbalize what you expect them to say aloud: "Thanks for helping with my homework, Mom." Occasionally I substitute "O Supreme Commander of the Universe" for "Mom." That always goes over well! But don't nag them to repeat your words. Eventually they'll internalize the manners you repeatedly model for them.

You can also provide objective information: "People like to feel appreciated when they help others," or "The Jenkins family believes in showing appreciation when others help us."

Modeling unrealistic entitlement

"I think it's ridiculous that my boss doesn't provide us with free parking!"

Instead of griping about what you think others owe you, keep it to yourself, or voice ways you think you can contribute: "The company doesn't provide free parking anymore. I guess the recession has really hurt their bottom line. I'll meet with the boss this week to go over some ideas I have for incentive programs that might boost employee productivity."

Praising only perfection

Praising perfection includes sticking only their A+ papers on the refrigerator door or singing praises for their most stellar accomplishments rather than the effort they put forth in the process.

Instead, concentrate on your child's successes—or even failures—that demanded a great deal of effort and perseverance. Even better, let your child decide what she thinks is praiseworthy. If she'd rather stick the thousandth turkey-hand on the refrigerator door instead of the A on her latest geography test, so be it.

Saying "I'm so proud of you"

This phrase may seem harmless, but it really tells children, "Let my level of pride act as the measure of your performance and therefore of your self-worth." It also invites sentiments like, "Yeah, but you're my dad. You have to be proud."

Try these alternatives that encourage children to assess their performance on their own: "I bet you're proud," or "You must be proud." Either one will get your child to decide if he is proud and, if so, what reasons he has for feeling that way.

When children know we will love and accept them no matter what they do or say, they feel at ease with us. From this comfort comes trust and admiration—two qualities that make us more effective guides. When they understand that, even though we may not always like their choices, we'll always love them, our children can welcome the guidance we offer rather than try to reinvent themselves to our satisfaction or whittle away at their self-esteem. This safety net of unconditional love encourages children to take chances they can learn from—a risk all heroes embrace.

Building self-respect

For your child to respect herself, show her respect. For instance, resist the temptation to fork things off her plate at dinner, enter her room without knocking, borrow her things without permission, interrupt her or not maintain eye contact when she is talking to you, or forget to introduce her to acquaintances you meet in public.

Most of us, including our children, work without producing tangible results. When we do our best as parents, it's reflected in our children's well-being, but there's no proof of it that we can hold in our hands, touch, smell, or see. Our children may do their personal best in school, but the knowledge and skills they gain are also intangible.

So we all need to stop and reflect with our child about what we've done recently that was commendable, even if it's as mundane as your daughter taking out the trash without being asked or your son making mom a cup of tea because she was tired. Without this reflection on what we've done to make a difference in the world, adults and kids can get stuck in the rat race, scurrying in our hamster wheels without appreciating our progress, and that is no good for a kid's—or adult's—self-respect.

So encourage your child to recognize, assess, and develop pride in her accomplishments, big and little. You can model this by keeping a journal of your own or recalling your accomplishments out loud. You can also encourage your child to write in her own journal of accomplishments at the end of every day. She might need your help recalling some of them at first, but eventually she'll look forward to the tradition.

From time to time, read it with her, discussing the value of each accomplishment and recalling both the effort it took and the obstacles she surmounted to achieve each one. Also, help her explore her unique set of strengths and talents and ways she can use them to contribute to different groups: her classmates, her friends, and so on. Open-ended questions are effective in inspiring the self-reflection necessary for this.

Some parents enjoy journal writing as an activity to share with their children. Not only does it provide children with the quality time they need with their parents, but it's also an opportunity to give and receive suggestions and reminders.

Self-respect also flourishes in positive peer environments. Not all peers influence our children negatively. In fact, children can help each other in many ways: by modeling responsible behavior, pressuring each other to make good choices, adopting healthy attitudes, providing objective feedback, and setting positive goals. Positive peer groups also encourage children to explore their limits and potentials—a key element to respecting themselves as human beings. That said, as parents we need to know about our children's activities and friends so that we can encourage positive peer relationships and forbid negative ones.

Learning to let go

Children are born helpless and small. Their very survival depends on our nourishment, love, comfort, shelter, and protection. So it's natural for us to consider ourselves their superiors. But over time, children's skills build and their needs diminish.

I've always had a hard time making that transition with my kids. As each infant grew to toddlerhood, I had to survive several episodes of their kick marks on my shins, patches of fur missing from my dogs, bowls of spaghetti hurling across the room like ground-to-air missiles, and their ear-piercing *"No!'s"* before I realized, "Hey, shouldn't I be disciplining this little fart?" It's not easy letting go of that infant stage and admitting that, yes, this child does have a mind of his own, he can make his own choices, and he is capable of handling more and more independence.

The same holds true for older children, too. For instance, a five-year-old should be capable of making his own breakfast. I'm not talking flapjacks, scrambled eggs, and bacon here, but he can pour his own cereal, make his own toast and butter it, pour his milk, and so on. Yet many parents don their apron and chef's hat to become their children's personal short-order cook. Who has that kind of time? Of course, you need to supervise your child, especially if his idea of breakfast is Pop Tarts, chocolate milk, and Laffy Taffy, or if he wants to prepare a breakfast that requires flames and breakables.

By the time your child is eight or nine, he should be able to do his homework and chores with little help or prompting. But I know scores of parents who hover over their kids like bees over honey, nagging them to get busy, giving them answers to their math problems, and coming up with sentences to use for their spelling words.

When your child is fourteen or so, there's not much you can do that he isn't capable of doing, too. OK, so he can't drive a stick shift, reconcile your bank statement — *I* can barely do that! — or land a lucrative job as a chemical engineer, but he can baby-sit younger kids, help paint a house, mow the lawn, and get the groceries — if he can hook a wagon to his skateboard, that is. In other words, kids aren't nearly as helpless as most of us believe. In chapter 10, we'll talk more about age-appropriate skills.

That said, though children may be smaller and less experienced, they are not inferior. Our superiority is limited to wisdom and experience, which we must use to guide them, not dominate or control them. Being a good parent means working ourselves out of a job. And that takes recognizing our child's potential and giving him every opportunity to reach it.

Why we use our superiority to our advantage and why we shouldn't

Being slow to recognize our children's growing independence isn't the only reason we capitalize on our sense of superiority. We also do so because it's effective. When it comes to getting a child to give his pigsty of a room a thorough cleaning, even turning him over to a gang of livid environmentalists wouldn't match a simple threat like "Don't you make me get the belt."

It makes our job so much easier—in the short run—to wield our size, strength, and authority over our children. But as effective as "abuse of power" parenting is in achieving obedience, sooner or later we have to pay the fiddler for these child-rearing shortcuts.

First, a "might makes right" parenting style is reactive rather than anticipatory, as it's often rendered when we're angry or frustrated rather than calm and analytical. Therefore, little time is spent figuring out the root of the misbehavior and finding strategies to guide our children. Our focus is to stop them in their tracks so *we* won't be upset with their behavior anymore.

Anticipatory parenting, on the other hand, involves seeing our child's misbehavior as a teachable moment rather than as something that vexes us. This viewpoint encourages us to calmly uncover the source of the problem so that we can better guide our child to understand why her actions are wrong, what she should do instead, and how she can stop herself from starring in reruns of the same misbehavior.

Control tactics have a "you against me" aspect that breeds resentment, shame, and anger in children. Some kids will compensate by developing effective manipulative tools that fuel the parent/child power struggles famous for bringing grown men—and women—to their knees.

Children subjected to consistent parental domination often become defiant and negative. Some even develop Oppositional Defiant Disorder, a condition in which children possess little respect for authority, act out with risky behavior, and show little or no remorse for their poor choices. On the other hand, some children react as shrinking violets who lack the self-confidence to find guidance from within. Their development remains at a standstill or even regresses. They don't stand up to negative peer pressure or the ridicule that comes from bullies who often choose kids like these as targets.

Households who rely on this parenting style are often plagued with conflict. Every relationship is tainted with hostility, and the entire atmosphere is heavy with both contention and negativity.

Control-free parenting: ten habits to break

Eliminating domination and control tactics is crucial to transforming our role from oppressive boss to mentor. Here are some examples of parental habits that prevent kids from finding their inner hero:

1. Threats and ultimatums

"You come here this instant, or you'll wish you did!"

"If you don't stop that right now, I'll give you a good reason to cry."

"Don't you make me get out of this chair."

Replace threats by one or more of the seven discipline techniques discussed in chapter 7.

2. Unfair or overly harsh punishments

"What? You got a C on your report card? You're grounded for three months, mister!"

"I want you to write 'I will stop plucking out Fluffy's whiskers' one hundred times. Stay in your room until you're finished."

"I don't care if you say you didn't draw pictures with my lipstick, you're getting a licking anyway. If you really are innocent, this is for all the things I *didn't* catch."

Discipline must be not only just, it must demonstrate a level of firmness appropriate for the crime. If it does not, children mount a counterattack or defend their pride rather than reflect on their behavior and find ways to improve it. Again, any of the seven empowering discipline techniques in chapter 7 would work well as replacements.

3. Illogical punishments

"I can't believe you tracked all this dirt in the house. You sit in the corner until I say."

"Since you borrowed my makeup without permission, no television for a week."

"I'm tired of you hitting your sister all the time. Come here and get your spanking."

When discipline makes little or no sense in relation to a child's misbehavior, two things occur. First, he feels resentment and lashes out in retaliation instead of contemplating his actions and its consequences. Second, the lack of logic confuses him instead of teaching him. Discipline must be logical for children to understand the consequences of their behavior so they can prevent its recurrence and make amends. Everyday heroes learn early on that every choice they make has a consequence.

4. Competitive contests

"Let's see who can get ready for school the fastest."

"I like the way Timmy is sitting so nicely in his seat."

"Let's see how fast you can get the paper. I'll time you. On your mark, get set, *go!*"

I hated getting rid of this one, because frankly, it worked so darn well. But using our children's innate competitive spirit just brings contention to the relationship between the competitors and fuels the winner/loser mentality so prevalent today. It's better to make your request politely and use one or more of the seven empowering discipline techniques if they refuse to comply.

5. Truth-seeking missions

I don't know of a single parent who hasn't resorted to the *"Vee haf vays of making you talk!"* technique. It disturbs us when our children tell lies, and we'll keep them under siege, using everything short of hot iron pokers and the rack to force a confession. But these tactics almost never yield results. In fact, children subjected to truth-seeking missions often learn to fear the truth and become more skilled in their sneakiness. So instead of exhausting them and ourselves with the third degree, try something like this:

"Who took my sewing scissors isn't the important issue here. I want them returned to their place or I'll have to take money out of everyone's allowance to buy a new pair. In our family, we show respect for each other's property."

"Both of you were in the garage when I got home. It's not important who painted pictures all over the walls there. You're both getting a bucket of soapy water and scrub brushes to clean it up. If one of you was just watching, it should have been your responsibility to stop the artist in his tracks."

I like this last one, because it inspires children to take care of each other and to be responsible, to some extent, for helping others make proper choices. An added bonus: the guilty party reaps the natural consequences he or she deserves—the ire of a lynching party. Furthermore, when we don't render a consequence to the "innocent bystander," we encourage our children to adopt the "every man for himself" or "Look out for number one" attitude, contributing to the winner/loser mentality that breeds hostility and isolationism in our society.

6. "Time crunch" remarks

"Hurry up! You're late for school."

"Stop dawdling, or I'll never get my shopping done!"

"Quick, finish your lunch, or we'll never make the movie."

Adding a sense of urgency to your voice occasionally lights a fire under kids, but more often than not, it only causes them to feel so anxious and upset that the pace of the entire family becomes frenzied. It certainly doesn't help them come up with ways to stay on time. In these cases, natural consequences work best. If your child is late to school, he gets a tardy slip. Most kids find this a mortifying experience. If she languishes over lunch and you have agreed to drive her to a movie afterward, either remove the food and take her to the movie, or say, "You seem to be taking a long time to finish lunch. We might not be able to make the movie today, but I'm sure it's going to be playing for awhile, so we can catch it another time." If your children dawdle during shopping, pack them back in the car and drop them off at the sitter's so you can finish your errands in peace. This may sound inconvenient, even counterproductive, but I can almost guarantee that their dawdling will be a thing of the past. You'll probably have to keep up with their scorching pace the next time you take them anywhere.

7. Degrading punishments

"You're being a very bad girl, saying words like this. I'm going to wash your mouth out with soap."

"You're a very bad boy. Go face the corner right now!"

Degrading punishments erode children's self-esteem and breed feelings of resentment and vengeance. Natural or logical consequences, along with other empowering discipline strategies, are tools that guide children's reasoning without tearing them down.

8. Unreasonable denials

My husband used to have a reputation as the "no man." My kids couldn't get past "Pappa, can we ..." without being cut off by a resounding "*No!*" It's easy to fall into this trap because, from toddlerhood on, kids constantly test their limits, skirting the edge of disaster or ruin. Our job is to protect them from their own inexperience, so halts, denials, and refusals seem to spew automatically from our mouths as if our mouths had minds of their own. But when we stop or deny children unreasonably or without hearing them out, they either get angry and retaliate or they feel powerless and stop reaching in life.

It's important to pause and ask yourself certain questions before you issue a denial: "Is the request reasonable? What's the worst that can happen if I say 'yes'? Can any good come from saying 'yes'? Will my child learn a lesson, develop more independence, acquire or hone a skill, or improve his sense of self?" You'd be surprised how many times your answers to those questions will turn a "no" into a "yes." Whenever a "no" is justified, back it up with a reasonable explanation—not only because children deserve it, but also because behind every explanation there's a lesson to be learned.

9. Negative words

Our penchant for reactive rather than anticipatory parenting prompts most of us to rely heavily on words that stop our children in their tracks—*if* the planets are aligned just right and we have our eyes crossed a certain way, that is. I'm talking about words like *stop, no, don't, quit,* and *can't.*

Since we're basically giving them a command, these words obviate our children's need to think at all. When they *do* think, it's rarely about whether they should change their behavior and why.

Their thoughts will be limited to "I wish Daddy would stop telling me what I can't do all the time," or "Why can't they just say 'yes' once in awhile," or "If she nags me one more time, I'm hitching a ride on the first banana boat to Outer Mongolia." Parents who use a lot of negatives with their children are setting themselves up for resentful, defiant children who rebel against parental oppression.

These words also train us to see our children in terms of their flaws rather than their strengths—what they do wrong rather than what they do right. Eventually this may take its toll on their sense of worth.

I'm not suggesting that you strike all negatives from your vocabulary. But in almost every instance, they can be avoided. Compare these two responses to a child's request to go outside and play: "No, you can't go out. You haven't finished your homework yet," and "Yes, you can go outside as soon as your homework is finished."

Instead of "Stop running along the dock! You could fall and hurt yourself!" try providing objective information: "Running along the dock is not safe." You could also let the kid slip and fall—unless the danger is too great—and then very sweetly say, "Gosh, Timmy, I'm so sorry you forgot our rule about running down the dock." Throw in a quivering lower lip and Timmy is definitely going to focus on the choice he made and how to prevent it in the future rather than lashing out at you.

10. Obstructions to communication

These little jewels are the phrases our parents used—and the ones we swore we'd never say when we became parents. (Why I told myself such a bald-faced lie is beyond me!) We often utter remarks that tell our children to shut their yaps because what they have to say isn't important. And we do this not just because we want an end to the verbal torture but because sometimes we run out of ammo and have nothing left to say! Some examples include remarks prefaced with "I don't care" or "It doesn't matter." For instance, "I don't care if you promise to be good; you're not going to Emma's party!" or "It doesn't matter, I still won't let you go to Eddie's."

If these remarks are your last defense against begging and whining, it's better to just say, "I don't feel the need to repeat myself." (You may have to repeat this over and over, firmly and calmly, until your child surrenders.)

Or you can respond to your child's nagging with an acknowledgment of her desire followed by a "nevertheless" and then a statement of your position. For instance, "I know you've been looking forward to hanging out with Eddie this weekend. Nevertheless, he's gotten himself into serious trouble with alcohol, and I'm not willing to risk your safety."

If the *"But Moommmmm's"* continue, keep repeating, "Nevertheless, I'm not willing to risk your safety."

Other obstructions to communication include the time-honored "End of discussion!" "I'm not listening to this," or my mother's favorite, "Period. Over and out!" I spent most of my childhood wondering if she was a reincarnation of Amelia Earhart, but the math didn't add up.

If you've had enough of the verbal tug of war, it's OK to say, "This conversation is going around in circles and is wearing me out. I've made up my mind and feel no reason to hash the same points over and over. If you come up with any compromises or arguing points that you think might be valid, write them down and share them with me tonight." (This last part is optional and should be included only if your decision isn't etched in stone.)

Encouraging children's unique insight

As I've said before, all children are unique, not only in appearance, personality, talents, interests, strengths, and weaknesses, but also in their thoughts. In order to help our kids become everyday heroes, we parents must give their unique outlook the room and permission it needs to develop on its own terms. Otherwise, a child's thoughts aren't really his own; they're someone else's. Without that sense of ownership, a child won't stand behind those thoughts and is not likely to feel accountable for any poor choices those thoughts may produce.

The fruits of a child's reasoning govern every choice she makes in life. Ownership of choices is the very thing that separates life's pawns from its players. Heroes are players. They know that each decision they make can either empower or enfeeble them. Children must produce, rely on, and have faith in their own thoughts in order to have mastery over their own lives.

Not telling children what to think

One sure way to rob a child of his unique insight is to tell him what he should think. When we do, it's the same as saying, "You don't know how to think for yourself, so I'd better think for you." Eventually, a child who is led to believe that his insights are flawed finds it difficult to trust his ability to form ideas and opinions and to transform those into self-directed choices.

Why do we do this? It goes back to our sense of superiority. After all, for most of our children's lives, we do know better than they. (Of course, the minute they reach adolescence, their IQs soar fifty points while ours plummet to moronic levels.) But rather than tell them what to think, we need to help them figure out where they stand on their own.

Following are examples of remarks that tell our kids what to think and of suggestions to replace them:

Thought invalidators

Thought invalidators dismiss children's opinions or ideas: "What are you talking about? You don't like Captain Crunch; you like Froot Loops. Don't you remember?" If you give your child a choice, allow whatever she decides, even if just last week she told you she hated Captain Crunch. If you don't, it never was her choice to begin with. It was yours.

Let's look at one more example: "You don't look frumpy in those clothes! I don't know where you got that idea. They're darling!" Perhaps the child is looking for comfort or validation, but belittling her opinion doesn't help.

Replace this invalidator with, "Gosh, I'm sorry you feel that way. Do you want to change before we go?" It's perfectly all right to express your disagreement with your child's opinion as long as we state it as our opinion rather than a fact etched in stone. For instance, you might say, "Personally, I think it fits fine, but the important thing is how you feel about it. Do you want to change before we go?"

Thought indoctrinators

Thought indoctrinators tell children what they should think: "You should be proud of this report card." As her parent, it's better to help a child figure that out on her own by asking, "How do these grades make you feel?"

Here's another example: "Don't be ridiculous. You don't hate your brother." Show your children that you have faith in them to work out their sibling quarrels by resisting the temptation to intervene. Whenever my kids squabble noisily, I toss them out in the backyard and say, "You can come back in when you've worked things out. Until then, I don't want all that racket disrupting my peace."

"Children are incapable of rational thought" suppressors

These suppressors tell children they can't make independent decisions by virtue of their status as children. When children truly are too little or young to take on a certain task, show them the logic that supports your decision and offer age-appropriate alternatives. Without a reasonable explanation, "You're too little" or "You're too young" make children angry or ashamed. If they blindly accept our point of view, their confidence in their ability to think independently can be weakened.

"I told you so" is a similar after-the-fact thought suppressor that tells children, "See! I told you to rely on me to make your decisions. As you can see by the mess you've caused, you're certainly not any good at it." Again, this undermines their faith in their ability to make choices, often to the point that they hesitate to make them at all—at least ones they consider important. This decision paralysis contributes to underachievement, failure phobia, and poor peer-pressure resistance. And believe me, if children don't make their own decisions, their peers will do it for them.

Finally, remarks or attitudes similar to "Children are to be seen and not heard" send the message that children in general are not mentally adept enough to make decisions, come up with ideas, and form opinions. Most of the time, phrases like this are uttered to avoid being bothered by the noise, idle prattle, and incessant requests so typical of children. But no matter how young they are, there are many age-appropriate decisions children can make. Even an infant can decide whether to smile or cry. And once they possess the necessary cognitive skills, even very young children can have their own ideas and opinions.

If you want your children to strengthen their reasoning skills and develop enough confidence to rely on their own choices, you have to give them the opportunity to think. Give age-appropriate choices as often as you can. Invite them to share their opinions about issues they can grasp—whether large or small—and try not to criticize or ridicule them when they do. Encourage them to share their ideas when solving problems or making plans. Though you don't have to adopt every one of their opinions or ideas, you can accept them as another point of view. By allowing our children to share their thoughts, we open up dialogue with them—dialogue from which they, and yes, even we, can learn.

Not pressuring children to conform

Insisting that children conform to standards formed by the media and pop culture tells them, "You have no business deciding your own taste in fashion and music or determining your own standards for appearance or behavior. Lucky for you, there are others out there who can make those decisions for you." This message saps their confidence in their reasoning abilities. Once they lose enough faith, they prefer to jump on the bandwagon rather than make their own conscious choices. And when they choose to react blindly rather than respond willfully, their resistance to peer pressure wanes.

Sometimes children express their uniqueness in ways that are so nonconformist it scares us. After all, most of us have been raised to be externally directed. What will people think of us when our kid leaves for school wearing army boots, purple socks, plaid shorts, and a paisley shirt? And we certainly can't bear the thought of our child being ridiculed by her peers for her fashion crimes! But the fact is, it's up to our children, not us, not their peers, and not society, to determine their tastes and define the standards they set for themselves.

Unless her clothes are so filthy that environmentalists are staging a protest on the front lawn or pigeons are hovering over her new punky hairstyle with nesting material in their beaks, let your child express her individuality.

Give guidance when solicited, but in a nonjudgmental way. For instance, if your child asks, "Do you think this shirt goes with these jeans?" you can respond, "Two types of stripes usually clash. Some people find that hard on the eyes because it's pretty busy."

Avoid statements that demand conformity: "You can't go to school wearing those shoes! Are you nuts? You'll be the laughingstock! Get upstairs and change right now."

Also stay away from complimentary remarks that encourage conformity: "You look so cute in those American Eagle jeans. I hear they're the rage now. You'll blow your friends away with that look!"

Shaming them into conforming is also a bad idea: "You're getting a little pudgy lately. I think you should go on a diet," or "You're not wearing your hair like *that*, are you?"

Try modeling your own individualism for your children. For instance, when I pick my kids up at school, I stick out like a sore thumb among the other moms. There they are with beautifully manicured nails, designer clothes, and costume jewelry, looking like they just came back from a garden-club luncheon. And here I am, shorts with frayed edges and spots of paint, my favorite "Stand for Children" T-shirt, no makeup, and nails that still have garden soil beneath them after repotting my bougainvilleas. Occasionally my kids offer comments and suggestions, especially when they feel the need to trail a hundred feet behind so no one will suspect the genetic connection. Nevertheless, I use that opportunity to assert my right to self-expression by saying something like, "I don't care what other people are wearing or how they behave in public. I do what I do and wear what I wear because I feel most comfortable that way. This is the real me. Take it or leave it."

Discouraging reliance on external beacons

It's a tug-of-war as we parents pull one end of the rope to encourage independent thought and influences outside the family and then pull in the other direction, telling kids to bypass their own reasoning. The struggle is tough enough as it is, so why do we parents sometimes let go of that rope and switch sides with bribes, rewards, or idle threats? Why do we invoke the opinions of other people, the prospects of having a punishment repealed, or the wrath of another authority figure to encourage our kids to act or be a certain way?

Tactics like these essentially tell kids that the decision to behave well lies in the outside world, not within them. This reliance on external beacons encourages children to precede their behavioral choices with questions like this one: "Is this the time it matters to be good or not?"

Where do they find the answer to a question like this? In the outside world:

"Mom looks pretty zoned out. She probably won't even notice."

"Dad's treating my brother OK, so he must be in a good mood."

"Mom says she had a rotten day at work. I'd better watch it."

In contrast, a child who relies on internal dialogue would precede her behavioral choice with questions like these:

"How will my behavior make others feel?"

"How would I feel if someone did that to me?"

"How will my actions affect me?"

Parents resort to external factors to get kids to behave because they work so darn well! Hold a lollipop over a child's head and the halo begins to glow. Threaten her with coal in her stockings and she stands at attention and salutes. Promise her a second chance and she falls at your feet like you've just pardoned her from death row.

To tell you the truth, this was a really tough one for me to give up. Imagine peeling my white-knuckled fingers off a winning lotto ticket and you get an idea. But I didn't want to make my children vulnerable to influences that they—and I—had no control over. And I certainly didn't want them to do the right thing only when there was something in it for them or to avoid punishment. Although such parenting tactics made my life a lot easier in the here and now, I knew they could set my children up for a bumpy ride the rest of their lives.

Parental no-no's

Bribes and rewards

Most parents admit to resorting to bribes or rewards. And the rest are just not being entirely truthful or are in the terminal stages of parental dementia.

We bribe children: "If you're a really good boy, I'll get you some Bubble Yum at the checkout counter," or "Stop crying, Pumpkin. I'll get you whatever you want if you just puleeeze stop embarrassing me!"

We offer rewards: "You got straight A's! Betty Lou, get my wallet. I'm giving this here genius fifty bucks!" or "Here ya go, Sport. A brand new BMX bike for having dry Pull-Ups for one month straight. Way to go, Buddy!"

When we use bribes and rewards, our children learn to manipulate us, and they grow into adults who rely on rewards to motivate them to do well or to do what's right. As parents, we must encourage our children to rely on healthier forms of motivation such as an understanding of positive and negative consequences of their behavior to themselves and others, their desire to honor their own values and principles, and their recognition that some choices must respect and uphold a greater good.

For example, I want my children to *want* to behave in the store because they respect others' right to a peaceful shopping trip, not because they fear my wrath. I want choices like these to be guided by benevolent selfishness, not external factors like bribes and rewards. In other words, since disturbing others would make my kids feel bad, to protect their own best interest, they'll settle down.

If my kids do pitch a fit in public, home they go. Then I turn that logical consequence into a teachable moment through dialogue guided by open-ended questions that help them reflect on the repercussions of their rowdiness on other shoppers.

Although the choices that affect children alone, rather than others, can't be guided by benevolent selfishness, they can be determined by internal rather than external factors.

For instance, I want my child to stop wetting his Pull-Ups because it's more comfortable sleeping in regular underwear. He should be motivated by a cold, wet, stinky Pull-Up weighing in at five pounds rather than by promises of toys, candy, and other rewards. (I take comfort in the fact that they won't be wearing Pull-Ups under their tuxes on prom night.)

I want my kids to make good grades because they enjoy learning; their grades are merely a reflection of that. They should be motivated by their intellectual gains and expanded potential, not by my pride or money or by having a better grade point average than their friends. When I see good grades on their report cards, I make a comment like, "Wow, by the looks of this A, you are really working hard in your history class! You must really enjoy it!"

In short, I encourage you to get rid of the bag o' bribes. Think of all the power struggles you'll avoid! And by not buying toys or candy every time you take your child to the store, you can book a cruise to the Fiji Islands with the money you'll save.

Invoking a higher authority

I used to use this one every chance I could. The last thing I needed during the holiday season was five wild beasts under my roof, torturing me with demands, whining, begging, fighting, crying, and resorting to other behaviors that made me wonder if they were all rehearsing for the lead role in *The Omen V*. In a desperate attempt to get them to behave, I'd threaten to call Santa to report every incident of bad behavior. (We had his secret North Pole hotline number.)

A conversation with the big jolly guy might go like this when one of my children refused to stay in bed:

"Um, hello, Santa. Look, I'm so sorry to bother you. I know how busy you are this time of year, but we're having a little trouble with Annika right now." (Annika's eyes are the size of Lifesavers now.)

"You see, she refuses to go to bed, and well, it's a school night." (Her eyes are now the side of poker chips.)

"Uh-huh. Yep. Uh-huh. Ooooh, so your list is still in the editing phase then. Still time to make changes, eh?" I say this into the phone while looking at Annika and nodding my head in a see-I-told-you way while pointing to the dead receiver. At this point, her eyes are the size of hockey pucks, and her mouth is not far behind.

"Wow, that's pretty serious then. Uh-huh. OK. Yes. Uh-huh. Oh, you want to talk to her? OK, let me see if I can get her to the phone."

By now, Annika's eyes are probably the size of dinner plates, but I wouldn't know, because she's in her bed hiding under her covers.

But why did she go to bed? Was it because she wanted to get a good night's sleep before school? Yeah, right. She was in bed because she wants toys, not coal in her stocking. And no kid in his right mind wants Santa to be angry with him.

So what could I have done instead? I could have told her that if she remained in bed, I'd check on her in five minutes, but if she didn't, I'd come back and turn off her lamp (as a logical consequence), explaining that a darker room would help her fall asleep. If she ignored my instructions, jumped ship, and scampered down to my room in search of a captive audience or a lively slumber party, I'd have to lock the door to my bedroom so she couldn't climb in bed with me. (It actually came to this. At first, she'd camp out at my door, but eventually she'd realize that her bed is a whole lot comfier than a cold, hard floor.) Another consequence could be making her go to bed thirty minutes earlier the next day to "catch up" on the sleep she missed.

Other "higher authorities" that parents commonly summon include "Wait till your father gets home!" the Easter bunny, the boogeyman, the devil, God, or that faceless man who lurks amid the shadows in every restaurant: "You'd better sit down or I'll have to call The Man," or "Eat all your broccoli or I'll tell The Man."

But whenever we invoke a higher authority to threaten kids, we tell them we can't handle them on their own, and we program them to rely on outside cues for guidance.

Using "other people" to get children to behave

Because desperate times call for desperate measures, there have been occasions when I've called upon the entire world's population to get my kids to behave well. Although I had infinite variations on the theme, the basic message was, "What will other people think?"

Some examples: "Stay still. There are other people here trying to eat in peace. Look at that couple over there. I've seen them looking at you. I bet they think you're a real brat," or "Can you imagine what other people might think if they heard you talk to me in that tone of voice?"

This approach basically uses shame to motivate children. Sure, it works sometimes, but then they learn to fear failure, seek the safety of conformity, and hand over guardianship of their self-esteem to other people — strangers, family members, and friends alike.

Allowing blame-shifting

Children often subtly transfer accountability to someone else. An example: "I can't help it. He made me angry!" I remember an incident in my childhood when I tried to pin part of the blame for my wrongs on someone else. My sister and I had caught some grass snakes and, armed with ice picks, were busily punching holes in the lids of the jars that were to be their new accommodations. As sisters will do, we were chatting up a storm. Since my attentions were elsewhere, I accidentally positioned the ice pick incorrectly so that when I pounded it with the hammer, it got buried in my thigh. My main concern was what kind of trouble I'd be in with my parents, so I cried out to my sister, "Look what you did! You made me hurt myself!" Unfortunately, my mom had me pegged and responded with, "What? Did she point a gun to your head? Did she hold a knife to your throat?"

When my children try to pull a fast one on me, I make sure they know that they and only they are responsible for the choices they make. Sure, there are times other people make it more difficult for us to choose one way or another. Nevertheless, our decisions belong to us, not others.

At times, we actually encourage our children to shift the blame for their mistakes to other people. When my children made a poor choice, I'd sometimes say remarks like, "I don't want you to hang out with that kid. She's a bad influence on you. She makes you get into too much trouble," or "He's no good. Look what he made you do!" But whenever I transferred part of the blame to someone else, I essentially told my kids that their decisions are steered by external forces rather than being under their complete control.

Other statements that encourage a poor sense of accountability in children include "You couldn't help it . . ." and "It's not your fault . . ." If you want your child to own up to his mistakes, avoid these at all costs.

Once children believe that outside influences take part in determining the choices they make, it's difficult for them to avoid repeating the same mistakes. After all, how could they feel responsible for something they can't fully control? If you do not want your child to associate with a certain child, a remark like, "I can't let you hang out with Mary anymore; you seem to make bad choices when you're around her," implies that your child's choice is her responsibility only. Instead of laying the blame on Mary, you let your child know that although outside influences can make it more difficult for her to choose wisely, her choice still belong to her.

Other parental remarks imply that the problems our children cause for themselves come from some outside source, thus encouraging them to rely on external beacons: "What made you do that?" or "What brought all this crying on?" Be sure your wording makes it clear that your child is responsible not only for his choices but also for the consequences they produce, good and bad. Replace these remarks with ones that reinforce full accountability: "Why did you decide to do that?" or "Why are you crying?" Such a subtle difference can make a big impact on whether our children control their behavior or not.

Idle threats

At times, I'm so exhausted that a herd of wild horses couldn't drag me off the sofa. Those horses are often my children up to all kinds of mischief. Since hope springs eternal, in the past I'd shout out threats that I had no intention of carrying out: "If I have to get off this couch, someone's going to be in big trouble," or "Don't you make me come up there."

Did my children know I was going to remain attached to that couch unless freed by surgical intervention? You bet. In fact, most children are so keenly aware of our bluffing that they know just how to make us fold our cards and to use our idle threats against us as manipulative tools. Some even turn them into a sport. Take the father sitting in his chair watching the Super Bowl while his kids are making shaving-cream designs on the windows. He hollers, "You kids clean up that mess and go upstairs to play. If you don't, I'm packing the whole lot of you off to bed!"

The kids refuse to budge because they're too immersed in their artistic creation. The father lifts himself off of his chair like a rocket leaving its launch, only to halt that launch a few inches above the chair the moment the kids run off, giggling.

The second he settles back into his chair, they go back to their art project. He does another aborted chair launch, temporarily getting them in gear, laughing hysterically as they scatter, but again, once he sits back down, they're back to their mischief. Guys like these have quadriceps the size of pickle barrels. It's a great workout, but it doesn't do much to take care of shaving-cream fiascoes and other forms of mischief.

So all we really accomplish with our idle threats is creating manipulative and highly entertained children. What would I have done, instead, in this case? I would have gotten up, made them clean up the mess, and driven them to the store to buy another can of shaving cream with their allowance. After all, if we *really* need to watch that show, there's always that little record button on the VCR.

Second, third, and even fourth chances
Most parents bail their children out of the very sentences they impose by changing the sentence to probation or

dismissing the charges altogether. Why do we parents become our children's overly lenient parole board? Sometimes we feel sorry for them. After all, they're pretty good at putting on the waterworks show, crocodile tears and all. Sometimes we had no intention of following through in the first place because the punishment we threatened would inconvenience us too much.

But when children are allowed off the hook time and time again, they tend to ask themselves, "What's the possibility of my getting another chance?" It doesn't take them long to search for clues to answer that question: "She gave me another chance yesterday, so maybe she won't today. Actually, she's kind of distracted now. Maybe she won't even bother punishing me." Once they're confident they can get away with a crime, they take full advantage of the opportunity. As long as we give them a reason to look for those answers from outside cues, their misbehavior will continue to smolder like a pesky fire in a tire factory.

In reality, children don't want to make the same behavioral mistakes over and over, because having disappointed or angry parents on their backs is no fun, even if threats of punishment never come to pass. And we certainly want to take the shortest, easiest, and calmest path to raising children who are sane, whole, and civil. That said, in the long run, holding fast to our initial sentence is more effective, because the misbehavior is quickly and permanently extinguished. When we haggle over the terms of a punishment, we encourage our child to rely on external factors. And replacing bad behavior with good goes a long way in building a healthy self-esteem and a strong inner compass.

Here's an example from my own experience. I remember a time when driving my five children anywhere was as pleasant as driving a car full of pigs to slaughter.

"How much longer?"

"Aarrrggggh, I'm dying of thirst!"

"Mommy, Erik is looking at me!"

"Get your elbow out of my space!"

"Hey, it's my turn to sit by the window!"

All this before I've even backed out of the driveway. It was enough to make me want to fire off SOS flares to signal passersby to come to my rescue.

Sure, I'd holler things like, "Don't make me turn this thing around" and a host of other empty threats, but the mobile torture unit prevailed.

One day I was struck by the epiphany that my usual strategies weren't making a dent now and, in fact, never had. I decided to set my kids up for a fall by cheerily announcing, "Guess what, guys, I'm taking you all to Astroworld!" If you only knew, as my kids do, how much I hate taking five kids to an amusement park in 110-degree weather so I can fork over hundreds of dollars for tickets, not to mention all the dough for drinks and goofy souvenirs they'll soon abandon as bookends or doorstops, then the shock on their faces wouldn't surprise you much.

With dumbfounded is-mommy-really-cracking looks, they quickly piled into the car, sat down quietly, and buckled their seatbelts. As we backed out of the driveway, I announced over their whispered prayers, "Oh, by the way, if there is any fighting or complaining back there, I'm going to have to turn back and go home. It just isn't safe to drive on the freeway with that kind of distraction."

I heard a collective sigh of relief that translated to "Oh, is that the only catch?" and they assured me that they'd be as quiet and well-behaved as church mice. As we approached the turnoff to Astroworld, I was biting my nails and sweating bullets, because my plan was backfiring! Everyone *was* being well-behaved! But thank goodness for small miracles and the nature of children—someone pinched, touched, elbowed, or squished someone else, and all hell broke loose. All I did—besides murmur a few prayers of thanks under my breath—was turn the car around and start for home. My kids were flabbergasted that I was sticking to my word even though we were a stone's throw from the Vomit Comet.

Despite their cries of disbelief and pleas for mercy, I stayed my course, fought back the urge to squeal with delight, and uttered an occasional remark like, "I'm sorry you chose to misbehave. You knew the rules, and once we make rules in our family, we stick with them. Perhaps we can try again another time."

There were one or two more incidents when I had to reinforce that same message: once on the way to eat lunch and once going to the neighborhood park. My kids made a fuss, and I turned back for home. Since then, you could host a reception for the queen in my car without twitching in anticipation of disaster.

By proving to our children that we intend to enforce the rules we make, unwanted behavior becomes a distant (but not too fond) memory and our lives become easier—and so do theirs.

Helping kids build skills to resist external beacons

One of the most challenging aspects of mentoring kids is helping them navigate and filter the peer and pop-culture influences they're bound to encounter. It is also one of the most crucial elements to raising a hero. Here are some strategies you can use to help your children find their way through that jungle:

- Role-play various scenarios of negative peer pressure or other outside influences with them. You can also use this to practice resistance strategies like walking away, calmly stating how they feel, using humor to disarm the tension, being assertive, or inviting peer mediation. Be sure to switch roles so they'll know what it's like on both sides of the fence.
- Help them find ways to contribute to their peer groups so they experience less pressure to fit in. Some kids adopt the mediator role in a group. Others might be talented at making their peers feel appreciated and accepted. Other kids enjoy helping their friends with schoolwork. Others are good at bringing objectivity to a problem or conflict. All children can carve out one or more meaningful roles within a peer group, and those roles can be different for each group they belong to.
- Use open-ended questions to help them understand the consequences to both themselves and others of succumbing to outside pressures, and discuss alternatives they can choose. Question-and-answer dialogue is highly effective at encouraging children to

reflect on their choices and the forces that sway them. Once they recognize those forces as something they can withstand, they are equipped to resist all temptations, both external and internal.

- Talk to your children about the same topics they discuss with their peers, and discuss the nature of life within the peer group in general, including trends, fashions, drugs, pregnancy, sexuality, and so on.
- Help them create lists of pros and cons so that they can figure out if following a new trend or a certain crowd is really the right thing for them to do, and if so, if it's a choice they'd make regardless of group consensus.
- Help them build sound conflict-resolution skills. To resist outside pressure, children must learn to stand up for themselves. First, help them understand the difference between assertiveness, passivity, and aggression. Assertiveness is firm yet positive. Passivity shows fear and makes them vulnerable, which only invites more pressure. Aggression is negative and demanding and is likely to create more conflict. Role-play each of these peer-resistance attitudes. Later, we'll discuss anger-management techniques that you can teach your children to rely on when attempts to resist peer pressure lead to conflict.

Encouraging responsible, conscious use of media

I don't know how many times my husband and I have gotten on our hands and knees to give a prayer of thanks to whatever god equipped my Suburban with a TV/VCR combo. We've stopped many sibling skirmishes and thwarted a host of annoying behaviors with this miraculous little electronic baby-sitter.

But before I booked my devotional pilgrimage to GM headquarters, I realized how irresponsible I had been in not exercising supervision and guidance for my children's contact with media. Many times I'd be too busy and preoccupied to worry about what video or television program they were watching. I wouldn't think of dropping whatever task I was engrossed in so that I could make sure the program was age-appropriate and in accordance to our family values. Truthfully, I was just grateful for a little peace and quiet! Every video and computer game was for me "a chance to weed the garden," "a moment in my bubble bath," or "a minute or two to catch up on my reading."

One day I was struck by the fact that, by not supervising my children's media exposure, I was essentially allowing a complete stranger to watch over and influence them. So my husband and I decided to compose a family media plan. We established rules and limits and created strategies to encourage our kids to use media intelligently and responsibly. Let me share some of them with you:

- We limit the time our kids watch television or play computer games to no more than one hour a day.
- That exposure must be nonviolent, creative, educational, and diverse, and it must reflect our principles and values.
- We encourage programming that invites our younger children's participation. *Blue's Clues* and *Sesame Street* are two examples.

- We try to use every opportunity to supervise what our children watch so that we can help them process and understand the messages and images they receive. Asking open-ended questions seems to be the most effective way of doing this.
- We like to watch educational or cultural programs together so that we can discuss them while strengthening family bonds.
- We always know the rating for whatever our children are reading or watching.
- Our children must ask permission to watch a program. Not only does this encourage them to see media use as a privilege rather than a right, it also gives us the opportunity to ask questions like, "Why do you want to watch that program?" or "Why do you want to play that particular computer game?" and to suggest other options like reading or playing outside.
- We make a point to express our disapproval for irresponsible media messages. For instance, if we're listening to the radio together and a song that goes against our family values begins playing, I'll turn it off and say, "I refuse to listen to that song because it's violent and degrades women."
- We establish clear-cut rules for media use outside our home and make sure other parents are both aware of and willing to honor them.
- We contribute financial support to our local public-broadcasting stations.
- We boycott violent programming and video games; irresponsible media that exploits women or portrays a distorted and destructive view of sexuality;

media that condones irresponsible, self-destructive, or immoral behavior; media that goes against any of our values, and so on. If the irresponsible media involves advertisements, we refuse to buy the product or use the service. Most importantly, we discuss our attitudes and actions with our children.

- We often encourage activities that don't involve the media.

Since we all have different opinions and values, tailor these suggestions to suit you and your family. Later, we'll discuss ways to involve our schools, our community, and the media itself in encouraging responsible media use in children.

Giving children space to struggle and learn

I've been guilty of thinking for my children on many occasions. For every "I'm bored! There's nothing to do in this house!" I'd come up with a flowchart of entertainment options in triplicate.

For every "Mommy, Kristina's picking on me!" I'd come rushing in to the fray like U.N. peacekeeping troops pouring into Bosnia.

For every messy room, unmade school lunch, or dirty breakfast dish, I'd swoop in like Mr. Clean on amphetamines until things were spotless.

For every "I want those new Adidas that look like cool alien shoes," I'd speed off to the mall, not even wondering for a moment if aliens really had feet, much less wore shoes.

For the first years of motherhood, I was social director, problem-solver, personal shopper, peacekeeping ambassador, and countless other roles that not only left me too exhausted to put my own last two remaining brain cells to use but left my children without a chance to exercise their own. During those years, I thought I was being the kind of parent after whom all others should model themselves, because I was doing everything I could to spare my little babies any discomfort or inconvenience.

The truth of the matter was that I found it easier to think for my children and provide their every need—to live their lives for them—instead of delegating that task to them. After all, being the obsessive-compulsive whirlwind that I was, I could handle their affairs so much faster and better than they could. Trying to get them to think on their own was far too inconvenient for me. I lived by the motto "If you want something done, do it yourself." And to expect them to satisfy their own desires was just as tiresome. Think about it. How easy is it to carry on with the day when bombarded by demands and pleas? It's much less painful to cave in to their torture tactics than to turn them into lessons that will make them strong and selfless.

How to stop rescuing kids

Rescuing children from reasoning or adversity shows an abject lack of faith in their ability to solve their own problems. And when they pick up on our sentiments, they learn to use our doubts to manipulate us, or they begin to lose faith in themselves.

When we start opening our minds to the possibility that children are capable of more hardship and introspection than we imagined, we can provide them with many opportunities to prove themselves. At first, we may think they'll fail, and perhaps they will, but success after success will turn our doubts into an undying confidence that they *can* do anything they set their minds and hearts to.

Let's look at ways to regain the faith in our children that they truly deserve. Here are some old habits for us to kick so that our children have opportunities to build both our faith in them and their faith in themselves:

Stop telling them what to do
Thanks to my penchant for efficiency, I've always had a problem with this one. Fortunately, the number of times per day I tell my children what to do has dropped from 246,790 to only 1,002. One look at the "Honey-Do" list I have for my poor husband and you'll see that he hasn't been nearly so lucky.

When children are subjected to continuous directives like "Erik, go get your mittens," or "Annika, come down for breakfast," or "Lukas, start your homework," they don't have to lift a single brain cell. They're on cruise control—Pavlov's theory, minus the drooling. Even when we issue these commands politely, it can still annoy our children into thinking, "My parents are such nags! I'm sick of them telling me what to do all the time." When they're thinking like this, they're not trying to come up with ways to anticipate our directives before we have a chance to issue them. Directives also let our children's issues become ours. They don't have to remember to take care of their mundane personal needs because they know we care about their cold hands, their late homework, and their uncombed hair. They know we'll remind them when something needs their attention. This lets them off the responsibility hook. They can cruise until the inevitable nag comes, and then they just follow orders.

What could we say instead? Here are the remarks above, reworded: "Erik, it's thirty degrees outside. What do you need to do to make sure you're comfortable at school?" or "Annika, breakfast is ready. The breakfast kitchen will be closed in fifteen minutes," or "Lukas, I see it's already five o'clock, and you haven't started your homework yet."

Statements like these get the cogwheels grinding in those little noggins of theirs until cobwebs fly off in all directions. When Erik rolls out the door looking like Nanook of the North, Annika dashes downstairs to eat, and Lukas rushes to the table, pencil in hand, it's because they made the choice instead of relying on others to prompt them.

Logical and natural consequences are also effective. Let Erik go to school without mittens, but call and let the teacher know he'll have to stay inside during recess. Have Annika skip breakfast if she doesn't make it in time. Let Lukas deal with his teacher's wrath when he doesn't turn in his assignments. There's nothing like consequences to exercise their brains.

When children do suffer consequences, turn them into teachable moments. For instance, ask open-ended questions that require a thoughtful answer:

"What's the rule about finishing homework?"

"Why do we have that rule?"

"What do you suppose would happen if there were no such rule?"

"What do you need to do to make sure you finish your homework on time?"

"So now how do you intend to make things right?"

When children complete a task without being prompted, point that out: "I see you thought to clean your room all by yourself," or "I didn't have to call you down to breakfast today!"

Stop rescuing them from boredom and frustration

Somewhere down the line, we parents got the idea that ensuring our children's satisfaction is part of our job description. But continually pleasing them requires us to rescue them from all their uncomfortable feelings, including boredom and frustration. This misconception must have evolved in a Darwinian manner, because there's something about that grating whine which makes it a powerful contraceptive device. Fearing what others might think of us if we don't ensure our children's contentment also contributes to our desire to rescue them from dissatisfaction. And considering how entertainment-hungry children are today, we tend to bend over backwards to resolve their boredom. We rush to them like a baseball player sliding into home plate when they voice the least frustration over a challenge they face. And if they want something—especially if "everybody else has it," all that comes to mind is our barefooted children in tattered clothes, selling matches on Tobacco Road in the snow. To avoid their tears or visits from Child Protective Services, we make fast tracks to the mall with credit card in hand. God forbid our children have to wait for or, worse yet, earn what they want.

Now when my children complain they're bored, I respond with one of these sentences:

"Do I look like your social director?"

"I'm sure you'll think of something fun to do."

"You know, it's good to be bored from time to time. It gives you time to think about things or to just relax."

"What a great time to catch up on your reading assignment!"

"Goody, I could use your help with spring cleaning!"

These last two normally get them scurrying for other options on their own! Now that I've stopped rescuing my children from boredom, their play has been incredibly creative. Once, after receiving no entertainment advice from me, they invented some game where they wore all their (clean) underwear on their heads so that the leg holes looked like goggles. Then they put all their socks in a sling-like gizmo and ran through the house, pelting each other with the socks. I think they were trying to play Darth Vader in Whitey Tighty Land. In any case, when one of my kids' friends showed up at the front door with his father, they both looked a little pole-axed. Finally the father said, "Gee, Elisa, I bet you have a whole chapter devoted just to this." Maybe I should.

When your children act frustrated while tackling a task, if you do anything at all, simply acknowledge their challenge. Keep your remarks limited:

"That looks really tough. I can see why you feel so annoyed."

"You've almost got it! I know you'll find a way to make it work soon."

Otherwise, leave them alone unless they ask for help. If they do, intervene only when you feel it's necessary.

You might ask questions to help guide them: "I wonder what would happen if you turned that piece the other way?"

Or make an impartial observation: "It looks like the base of the tower is too narrow to support the other blocks."

Try to discourage statements like "I can't do it," because this implies they're helpless. Instead, encourage them to say, "I need a little help."

When the task is obviously something they can handle on their own, respond to their requests for help with encouragement: "I know you can do it as long as you keep trying," or "You've always been a great problem-solver. I have faith in you to figure things out on your own."

If they're frustrated, recommend they leave the task for a while and come back to it when they feel more relaxed: "You might have an easier time with that if you take a break for a few minutes. Do you want some lunch now?"

Stop rescuing them from unrequited desires or delayed gratification

Not rescuing children from unrequited desires or delayed gratification gets easier if you picture the greenbacks being flushed down the toilet when you satisfy their yearnings. It also helps to remember that we hurt our children by giving in to their unreasonable demands. Children need our guidance to develop patience, tolerate unfulfilled desires, and develop a realistic view of what they're truly entitled to have and what they must earn on their own.

I knew I was in trouble when I asked my then four-year-old son what he wanted to be when he grew up, and he replied, "A king." It confirmed my suspicions that I was raising a bunch of kids with an overblown sense of entitlement when I asked him how he intended to earn a living, and he responded, "Like this," thrusting his hand out, palm up. Since then, I've made some changes in my child-rearing practices, and things do seem to be improving. That same kid, now thirteen, has settled for becoming a general in the army once he graduates from college.

In our family, our children earn every dime they have. Part of their money is put aside for long-term savings, part is put aside for charity, part is put aside for intermediate-term purchases, and a small amount is left for fun splurges. They're completely responsible for their discretionary spending, including occasions when they want to make a purchase that exceeds my budget for that item. For instance, if I normally spend $30 on athletic shoes for a child, he pays anything above that from his own coffers. If they whine because there's this new Playstation 2 game they can't live without, I defuse the mounting tension with a little humor by asking, "What, is it your birthday already? How did I let that one slip up on me? Or wait a minute, could they have changed Christmas to July?" Well, at least *I* think it's funny. Other times, I just ask, "Can you afford it?" That usually shuts them up right away.

Consider instituting a family rule that discourages immediate gratification. If your child has his heart set on a big-ticket item, have him wait at least two weeks to purchase it. If children beg for some new toy or fashion, make sure they know it's their financial responsibility by saying, "Sure, you can buy it, as long as you have enough money and you wait out the two weeks."

When children are fifteen to sixteen years old, encourage them to develop budgeting skills. Give them a certain amount of money per month. From that, they must pay all their expenses (other than room and board and family outings like movies, dinners out, or vacations). Leave it up to them to budget money for haircuts, clothing, school supplies, social outings with friends, passport renewals—you name it. All of a sudden, shopping at Target or Kmart isn't so "retarded." Ten-dollar haircuts are just fine. Skipping an outing to Starbucks with their buddies is bearable. Wearing $25 tennis shoes is not so "uncool." Eventually they'll develop the shopping prowess of Scrooge. My teenage daughters know how to sniff out every factory-outlet store for a bargain, and they don't hesitate to sing their own praises when they come across a great deal.

In short, children are capable of tolerating boredom, coping with frustration, delaying gratification, and doing without. Over time, they handle these things on their own without complaining or asking us to intervene. It becomes a new reality for them—and a more manageable one for us!

Refusing to rescue children is not enough to empower them to become everyday heroes, however. Leaving them to their own devices is useless, even harmful, if it is not accompanied by our guidance. When your child suffers the discomfort that boredom, frustration, or longing brings, help him reap the lessons to be learned through that adversity.

For instance, if you refuse to let your child requite his burning desire for the latest Playstation game, you could guide him in the direction you want him to go with questions like these:

> "Two weeks ago, you were really drooling over that new James Bond game I wouldn't let you buy. How do you feel about it now? Do you think you'd regret the purchase?"

> "You've saved yourself fifty bucks. That's money you can save toward your first car. How will you feel when you earn your first set of wheels by yourself?"

Questions can also help guide your child when he struggles to find solutions for boredom or frustration.

Any objective feedback that inspires inner praising can reinforce your child's success in solving problems: "I really admire the willpower you showed by not forking over a big chunk of change to buy that game. That required strength I don't often see in adults. You must be proud." Do the same when they overcome boredom or frustration.

Stop rescuing them from problem-solving, conflict resolution, and other challenges

Children are quite capable of solving problems, meeting challenges, and working out differences with others, as long as they have the tools to do so and as long as the challenge is age-appropriate. Only a parental lack of faith prevents them from practicing these crucial life skills.

Resist the urge to solve your child's problems for her. Intervene only with feedback, guidance, and encouragement. Suppose your child wants to be in Girl Scouts again this year, but her best friend is dropping out. Use questions to help guide her:

"Why does she want to quit?"

"Is there any way you can change her mind?"

"What do you plan to do if she refuses to reconsider?"

"What other friends will be in your troop?"

"What are the pros and cons for deciding to stay versus dropping out like Sarah did?"

Also offer acknowledgment and comfort: "I'm sorry she decided not to stay. I know you two are such good friends. You must be pretty sad about her decision. No matter how hard things seem now, I know you'll handle it well. And whatever you decide to do, you have my support."

When your child struggles with a problem, resist the urge to explain its nature and how to solve it without first letting her have a stab at it. Here's an illustration of rescuing through explanation: "The reason you can't get your zipper up is you don't have the ends lined up. Line them up and pull the zipper down over them. Then try zipping up." To avoid overexplaining, replace these remarks with a suggestion: "It looks like the ends don't match. I wonder how you could fix that?"

Don't rescue your child in advance by assuming she doesn't have or won't remember the knowledge needed to prevent or solve a problem: "Now, remember, you have to mix the dry ingredients together before you add the milk," or "Be sure you wear socks under your rubber boots, or you'll get blisters."

Sometimes we try to spare children interpersonal conflict with friends, siblings, and other people. Sibling rivalry is enough to push us off the deep end, so the minute our second child is born, we hone referee skills that would qualify us for the NFL. But when you intervene in relationship problems, you not only deny your children the opportunity to develop conflict-resolution skills, you also arm them with one more weapon of manipulation that can catapult parent/child power struggles to new levels.

Staying out of his conflicts doesn't mean you shouldn't teach your child techniques to voice his anger constructively. Anger should not be suppressed. It communicates to other people behaviors we will not tolerate. The healthy approach to conflict below relies on assertiveness. It stresses that name-calling and insults only widen the rift and defeat the purpose anger is meant to serve. This approach includes four steps:

1. First, teach your child to say he is angry in a firm tone of voice, using "I" messages: "I'm very mad at you!"
2. Then, he should indicate why he is mad, based on one of two root emotions: fear or hurt. Anger is not really a root emotion. Fear or hurt always underlie it: "It hurts my feelings when you talk about me behind my back," or "I'm afraid you're going to hurt me if you keep tripping me in the halls."

3. Next, your child should state his expectations: "I want you to stop spreading all those false rumors," or "I want you to stop tripping me from now on."

4. Last, he should insist on an acknowledgment: "Can you agree to that?" or "OK?"

Once you teach your children this approach for expressing anger, they will grow stronger with every relationship instead of destroying old bonds or squandering opportunities to build new ones.

When my children have an irreconcilable difference, I make them sit down and go through these steps until they're both satisfied. At first, I needed to be there to mediate, but now they follow the steps on their own.

What do you do when your children appeal to you to settle their conflicts? If it's a situation they can handle on their own, you might respond, "I have faith in you to handle this on your own," or "You two were getting along so well yesterday. What's different today?"

No matter what, make it clear that solving their disagreements is not more important to you than it is to them. And as I've mentioned before, if their fighting disturbs the peace, don't hesitate to shoo them outside or into another room until they've worked things out. Until they do, their lives are on hold, entertaining activities notwithstanding.

Children who are allowed to work out their differences with others generally form healthier and longer-lasting bonds throughout their lives. They also get needed practice in valuable skills such as compromise and negotiation.

Sheltering children from challenges is a parental form of damage control — putting out fires before they start. Many parents discourage their children from sports or other challenges because they don't want to set them up for failure. I say, "Set 'em up for as many falls as you can."

During childhood, failure is not as likely to sting as hard or as long as it might later on, because the risks are relatively lower. Whether or not they excel in ballet is not as crucial as whether they succeed in their career. Furthermore, failure deals a softer punch when we parents are there to pick them up, dust them off, and hug them.

So when your child wants to take on a challenge, or when you come across an activity that might put her talents to use or explore the sincerity of her interests, by all means encourage her to meet that challenge. What better way to build skills like initiative, problem-solving, and persistence? And what better way for a hero in the making to test her limits and expand her reach?

Lastly, when your children solve a problem, settle a conflict, or overcome a challenge, point it out:

"You figured out how to complete that puzzle all by yourself!"

"I see you and Bobbie worked things out on your own."

"Trying out for the football team took a lot of courage. You must feel proud."

Whether they fall short or not, with your guidance, your children can still learn valuable lessons when you ask them thought-provoking questions:

"What part of that problem/challenge/conflict did you think was most difficult?"

"What would you have done differently?"

"What knowledge or skills did you acquire by taking this on?"

Stop rescuing them from the consequences of their mistakes

Most parents confess to bailing their children out from time to time. After all, when we're the ones who have to deliver the consequences for our kid's transgressions, it can be pretty inconvenient. When others, such as a police officer or teacher, impose those consequences, we often feel the need to come to our child's defense with pleas, demands, and excuses.

Regardless of who's delivering the consequences, it's hard to stand back and watch as your child suffers under them. But children should experience consequences for their mistakes, whether intentional or not. They should learn that everything they do has some sort of consequence. After all, when they're young, those consequences are a real bargain compared to the ones the adult world renders. Compare the parental consequence, "Megan can't come over to play, because you treated her badly at the park yesterday," to consequences she might receive as an adult, such as, "You're fired" or "I want a divorce." And when they're still children or adolescents, we need to be there to offer comfort and support and to help them reap the lessons to be learned.

So when your child repeatedly forgets to take her backpack to school, let her deal with whatever consequences the school delivers. When he makes a bad grade, don't call the teacher to beg for leniency. When he dawdles in the morning, let him get a tardy. When she refuses to share a toy, let her experience the anger of her playmates or the loss of a friend. You could even help come up with consequences for your child to prevent repeat mistakes. For instance, when she forgets to log her assignments in her student planner three times in a row, ask the teacher to give her a lunch detention.

Here's an example from my own experience. One of my teenage daughters has, like me, the depth perception of a myopic cyclops. Three days after she received her driver's license, she crashed into a pole. Did I pay for the repairs? Nope. I left it up to Allstate and her. Insurance took care of all but the $500 deductible—a considerable chunk of change for a sixteen-year-old to earn. We're talking hours and hours of baby-sitting. Two months later, she had a second fender bender that put her in the hole for another $500. Again, she was able to earn it all by baby-sitting and pressure-washing all of the neighbor's belongings other than their pets and kids, but she also lost her insurability. As a result, she won't be able to drive for two to three years—the kiss of death for today's teenagers. But I'll bet my firstborn that when she does get behind the wheel again, she'll drive with the precision of the White House chauffeur. Not only that, she can now wield that pressure-washer like a blindfolded gunslinger.

Whenever your children suffer the consequences of their own mistakes, seize the opportunity as a teachable moment. I helped my daughter examine the consequences of her driving mistakes by using open-ended questions:

"I'm so sorry you have to pay so much money to get the car fixed. I can see how that makes you feel disillusioned and angry."

"What do you think contributed to the accident?"

"What do you think you could have done to prevent it?"

"When you drive again, what changes do you plan to make to lessen the chance of having another accident?"

This parental dialogue acknowledged her suffering, showed acceptance for her feelings, and modeled compassion and empathy.

So have faith in your children to deal with the consequences for their mistakes. They'll sense your faith, develop skills that will help them cope, and more important, they'll learn to anticipate potential consequences prior to making their choices.

Stop rescuing them from responsibility and commitment

Have you ever taken care of your child's chores or responsibilities because it was a whole lot easier than getting him to do it or dealing with the griping that would be sure to result?

Have you ever allowed your child to back out of a commitment because you just didn't have it in you to insist she stick with it? I've sure been there, done that. My older two kids got off easy, because my idea of chores was for them to do their homework, toast their own Pop Tarts, and push the buttons on the television remote. As for commitments, I rarely encouraged them to make them, much less insist they honor them, because the last thing I wanted was something else to remind them to do.

Many kids go through their entire childhood and adolescence without lifting a finger to do chores, take care of personal responsibilities, or make and keep commitments. Were it not for parental intervention, some children would wear clothes smelly enough to signal the National Guard, would starve to death before fixing their own lunch, and would forgo teeth-brushing until their teeth were riddled with cavities the size of potholes.

When a child is rescued from responsibilities and commitments, she develops a warped sense of entitlement, fails to develop the practical skills of life, misses out on the satisfaction that comes from contributing to others, and fails to develop the self-confidence that comes from making valuable contributions.

Not only should we require our children to fulfill age-appropriate responsibilities, but we shouldn't feel obligated to pay them for these contributions. Although I give my children a small allowance, I let them know that what they get represents a share of the family's income. It only stands to reason that, as a contributing member, they should reap some of the family's earnings. My children consider chores their contribution to the whole, and their reward is the satisfaction they get from feeling valued. If I ask them to do something more, I do not pay them any additional money. This—thankfully—includes baby-sitting.

Encourage your child to make and keep their commitments. For instance, if a child of mine tries to back out of a baby-sitting job in favor of party plans, I'll respond, "We keep our promises in our family. You're a Medhus, so you're sticking with the commitment you've made."

If they balk, I not only forbid them to go to the party, I make sure they apologize to the appropriate person for even contemplating the idea of backing out, and I make them baby-sit for free. Then I use questioning to make sure they understand the importance of honoring commitments:

"How do you feel when someone breaks a date with you?"

"How do you think others feel when you break a commitment?"

"What do you think they would have had to do if you canceled out on them with such short notice?"

One caveat: It's perfectly fine to help your child out by doing an occasional chore for him when he is swamped with homework or by bringing a missed assignment to school the first time or two that he forgets. After all, we need to model compassion and generosity, and they need to learn that families are there to help each other out.

Encouraging introspection

Now that you've learned ways to enhance your child's reasoning, let's look at ways you can inspire it. First, model your own thought processes by sharing your opinions, ideas, and beliefs with them.

Second, regardless of how old they are, ask your children to share their thoughts with you. My parents were very special in this regard. Even when I was just five years old, they'd sincerely ask my opinion about certain fairly important matters. Of course these were age-appropriate, but nonetheless, being asked my opinion gave me confidence in my ability to think critically. Encourage your children's involvement in family discussions by asking for their input and advice.

When your child does share his innermost thoughts, whether you agree or not, never dismiss, belittle, or contradict them. Instead of saying, "That's wrong. I'm certain El Niño causes more rain in the West," try saying, "I always thought it caused more rain in the West, but I could be wrong. Let's read about it. Maybe we'll both learn something new."

The third way to encourage introspection is to provide positive feedback when your child expresses her thoughts: "I admire the courage you showed when you shared your feelings," or "You really seemed to put a lot of thought into this! It shows!"

Fourth, resist the temptation to allow your child a phone, television set, or Internet access in his room. I've seen the harmful effects on my own children—effects that took a great deal of time and effort to reverse. Children immersed in these passive forms of interaction seem to never come out of their rooms. When they do come out, all pale and glassy-eyed, it's usually only to eat, ask for money, or pester their siblings. Before long, they've gone through puberty behind their bedroom door without our knowledge.

Once I realized what a mistake I'd made, I wasted no time ripping these hypnotic devices from their rooms. After a while, my kids started to come out of their caves like zombies on a midnight march and slowly but surely learned to interact with the rest of the family again—to bond, listen, discuss ideas, and share their lives with us.

Last, we can encourage our children's reasoning by question-and-answer dialogue, role-playing, pros-and-cons lists, and so on.

How to send clear messages to children

Although sometimes children seem to have been put on this earth to confuse us, sometimes it's the other way around. Some things we parents do muddy the cerebral waters for our children. When we're not clear in our language and rules, it becomes difficult—even impossible—for kids to generate the internal dialogue to make a responsible choice.

Avoid double standards

How many times have I heard my husband tell one of our teenagers, "Dammit, stop cursing!"? Plenty of times. Parents often have a different set of behavioral standards for their children than they are willing to follow themselves, because—let's face it—those standards are usually pretty high. To abide by all of them might call for a lot of habit-kicking. In this cursing example, the teenager is apt to come up with all sorts of excuses and rationalizations for her foul language: "Gee, my old man cusses a blue streak and he's pretty cool. I guess that rule was really made for other people," or "If Dad curses, then I can too. I don't care what he says."

Don't set unreasonable rules and boundaries

As children grow, some rules and boundaries we have set for them need to change. After all, we can't expect our five-year-old and our fourteen-year-old to have the same bedtime! (But yes, sometimes I'm tempted to make my teenagers go to bed earlier than my younger ones!)

If you want your children to comply with your rules because they agree that the rules are the right thing to do, not because they fear the consequences, then you have to set reasonable rules. When kids agree with rules, they're less likely to get upset about them. Confusing rules and boundaries breed resentment—"What does she think I am, a baby?"—and external direction—"I guess I'd better do what he says. I'd hate to be grounded again."

List those rules you believe are reasonable, go over them with your children to get their input, and explain the importance and rationale for each rule. Then make sure the entire family reviews and, if necessary, revises that list on a regular basis. As children change, so should family rules.

Avoid wishy-washy parenting
Some parents squirm at the thought of exercising parental authority because they want to be liked by their children—to be their friend rather than their guide. Here are some common examples of wishy-washy parenting:

- *Pleading.* (I know some parents who have calluses on their knees for this very reason.) When you say, "Please stop being so rough with the dog," as your child is holding it up by the ears, you're letting her know that continuing to behave like that is an acceptable option you hope she'll consider. *Pleases are designed for requests for assistance, not obedience.* Instead, try giving a choice: "You can either treat the dog nicely or we can give him away to someone who will." Or try providing specific information: "We don't allow animals to be mistreated in our family." Or try delivering a logical consequence: "I can't let you play with Peanut until I'm sure you'll be gentle with her."

- *Negotiating.* (Colin Powell, eat your heart out.) The way many parents discipline their children, you'd think they were spearheading a revival of the old "Let's Make a Deal" television game show. Negotiating is fine when reexamining rules, boundaries, and responsibilities, but it has no place in a discipline program. If your rules are clear and reasonable, your children should comply without contingencies. So instead of saying, "Look, the last time I let you borrow the car, you didn't go where you said you'd be. But I'll make a deal with you. You can take it this one time if you give it a good wash and wax and if you trim the azaleas Saturday. Wanna shake on it?" you can say, "Because you weren't where you promised you'd be, I can't let you borrow the car until you regain my trust. We'll see how dependable and responsible you are in other areas of your life first."

- *Needless lecturing and explaining.* (See dictionary for *Congress*.) Yada, yada, yada. The more oral diarrhea we subject our children to, the more they tune out. My husband, an immigrant from Norway, used to give his infamous "When I was your age, I walked ten miles to school every day, uphill both ways" speech whenever one of the kids complained about anything requiring them to exert energy. Within seconds, their eyes would glaze over (probably exhausted from all that rolling up inside their heads at the beginning of his lecture), and it was obvious their minds were elsewhere. This gives credence to the whole astral-projection concept. So if your child gripes about riding his bike to school, tell him, "You can either go on complaining and be tardy or you can start pedaling and make it before the bell rings."

- *Ending requests with "OK?" or "Alright?"* When you say, "Don't run off like that in the grocery store, OK?" you're basically asking your child for permission to parent him. Better alternatives are, "You can either stay by the cart, or we can go home now," or "Running off in public is not safe," or "If you come back and stay where I can see you, then we can stay and continue our shopping."

- *"I give up" phrases.* When they hear phrases like "I just don't know what to do with you" or "I give up; nothing seems to work with you " not only do our children think, "Oh goodie! I can get away with murder, now!" they learn that "making Mommy reach the end of her rope" is an effective manipulation tool. But deep inside, they wonder why they're not worth the effort necessary to help them behave. If you truly are at a loss for discipline approaches, tell your child, "I'm really upset right now. I need a few minutes to collect myself before I decide what to do about your behavior." You can also ask him to step into your shoes for a moment: "If you were the parent in this situation, what would you do to resolve it?" Although children test their limits, they truly do want clear rules and boundaries that are enforced firmly and consistently. Wimpy parenting causes them to feel uncertain about themselves, their parents, and the unstable lives they live.

Ignore inner dishonesty

Sometimes kids' excuses and justifications are as obvious as a flashing neon sign. Yet we parents often let their inner dishonesty slide because it takes effort from us to call them on it (particularly when a showdown is certain), or we don't want to think of them as having flaws, or we don't want to hurt their feelings, or we want to justify their problem just as much as they do. But by not confronting every attempt to rationalize, excuse, or deceive themselves or to finger somebody else for the crime, we allow that inner dishonesty mechanism to become stronger and stronger until, eventually, their inner guardian doesn't stand a chance.

When your child is not honest with herself, call her bluff. For instance, when Jessica reneges on going to a party she's been excited about for weeks, giving the excuse that Mary's parties are always so dull, you could respond, "You seemed so thrilled about going yesterday. I have the feeling there's something you're not sharing. What's happened since then?"

Jessica answers, "OK, you're right. I'm really upset, because one of my friends heard Mary telling someone she's only inviting me because she has a crush on my brother. She said I was a total loser!"

You might respond, "It took a lot of courage to admit that to me and to yourself. And although I know that really must have hurt your feelings, do you think hiding from the problem is the only solution?"

Jessica replies, "I guess I should let Mary know I'm on to her motives and that she really hurt my feelings with her comments."

You say, "That sounds like a great idea. Who knows, maybe the whole thing is a misunderstanding that can be cleared up in a snap. If not, at least Mary will know what kind of behavior you refuse to tolerate."

Once your child realizes that you won't let him pull the wool over his own eyes any more than you'll let him pull it over yours, he'll know the enormous relief that comes from being honest with himself and the refreshing self-clarity that results.

By becoming the mentors our children need and deserve, we can guide them with love, faith, and clarity. Our love, unconditional and objective, is the mirror that reflects the treasures within them, obvious or hidden, now or in the future. Our faith in their potential is the fire that inspires them to stumble and then get back up and try again, to take on difficult or arduous challenges that build strength and skill, and to define their unique personalities, preferences, insights, and goals. Our clarity is the messenger that delivers our words of guidance, faith, and love in unequivocal terms—terms that honor our resolve to bring them up as heroes. Together, these three are the lamps that will light our children's way.

10

Mentoring Children toward Adulthood

The most important thing that parents can teach their children is how to get along without them.

—Frank A. Clark

If we're going to raise lifelong heroes, we can't very well pitch them out of the house the minute they turn eighteen, lock the door, mop the sweat from our brow, heave a sigh of relief, or perform the Bakwena Tribal Dance of Joy unless we've prepared them for life in the adult world. It's one thing to engender self-direction and independence when they're children, but without practical skills, their heroism will disappear faster than a ferret up a trouser leg.

We must not leave the task to schools and other outsiders. Preparing our children to become happy, productive, and contributing adults is ultimately up to us alone. In this chapter, we'll explore ways to encourage their independence. Then we'll discuss transitional skills we can help our children acquire so that their passage into adulthood is smooth, unlike the abrupt kick in the teeth it is for many young adults. After that, we'll discover ways to help children, at various stages of development, create a life plan. And finally, we'll explore ways to help them become contributing adults.

Encouraging independence

We've looked at parenting strategies that encourage self-reliance. Now here are twenty parental habits that can foster independence in your child:

Avoid pessimistic language that fosters dependence

Many common phrases actually discourage independence in children. Sometimes we say things that reflect our lack of faith in their potential. Sometimes we are just expressing our desire to help the ones we love. Other times, our perception of their abilities lags behind what they're truly capable of doing, so that we can't picture them handling a particular task successfully. When we say such phrases, we tell them not to spread their wings and grow—that it's acceptable to remain in a stagnant state of dependency. Here are some examples as well as alternatives that encourage independence:

Instead of "That won't work," say "It's worth a try."

Instead of "You can't do that by yourself," say "I can help you if you want."

Rather than "You won't be able to reach that," try "That's pretty high up. Let me know if you need any help."

Instead of "You can't possibly lift that by yourself," try saying "I can help you lift that if you think it's too heavy."

Accompany independence with responsibility

When your child engages in a task that shows his self-sufficiency, make sure he accepts the responsibility that goes hand in hand with it. As I sit here clanking away clumsily on my laptop, I've only to turn my head forty-five degrees to see the science lab that's become of my kitchen. Lukas, my ten-year-old, has seven different experiments in process—from making a stalactite, to studying the way plants bend toward light, to checking various liquids (some of which I can't recognize and am really not sure I want to) with his homemade hygrometer.

I try never to obstruct the explorations of his creative mind, but the rule is this: He must clean up after himself and leave me at least two square feet of counter space on which to prepare meals.

Most thirteen-year-olds, once they understand and demonstrate the appropriate safety practices, should be able to use the family tools as long as they take good care of them and put them in their proper place when they are finished. Those responsible enough can even use power drills and saws with supervision. Taking this leap of faith provides an opportunity to learn vigilance, responsibility, and respect for other's property.

One more example on how to encourage independence that's backed by responsibility: Say your five-year-old spills some milk as she's struggling to pour some into her cereal. Instead of taking over the task, fussing at her, or cleaning up the mess yourself, respond by saying, "I noticed you poured the milk all by yourself. That's a pretty heavy carton for a kid your age to lift, but you only spilled a little bit. Here's a rag to clean whatever didn't make it into the bowl."

Encourage your child to do things on his own
Some children are born with a thirst for independence. Others have to be nudged a little. When your child is reluctant to take on a task you feel she's capable of doing, help her take the leap with words of support and encouragement, and let her know it's OK to mess up. If she does fail, point out what she did well in the task. When my eldest son was learning to write his letters, he really struggled. He inherited his mother's indecipherable, chicken-scratch handwriting that looks more like Sanskrit than English. I watched as he wrote an entire line of lower case *e*'s in his writing tablet. Most of them were

way off the mark, but when I found one that was pretty close, if you squinted just right, I said, "Wow, look how the bottom of this one hits the line perfectly. And you got the top of it to hit the line as well!" After that simple remark, the rest of his *e*'s were at least as good! Some of them looked like they were typewritten. All of them put me to shame.

Remain the ever-supportive spectator
Children learn more by doing a task than by observing it being done for them. Of course, if your child has no idea where to begin, you can give her some instruction, but then resist the urge to take over when she struggles at a task. Instead, encourage and guide her. For instance, say your daughter decided to make beaded friendship bracelets as Christmas presents for all of her classmates. After one or two are finished, her fingers start to get stiff, beads slip off the string, and she breaks down in tears of frustration, crying out, "These stupid bracelets! Why did I ever decide to make them? I'll never get them finished by tomorrow! I hate them (*stomp*)! I hate them (*stomp*)! I hate them (*stomp*)!"

At this point, restrain yourself from rescuing her from the project by taking it over. Instead, acknowledge her feelings: "I'm sorry you're having such a hard time, Sweetie. I can see how stringing all those beads could be frustrating. In fact, I'm amazed you did the first few so quickly." Perhaps offer a suggestion: "Maybe it would help for you to take a short break every time you've finished a few. After you've rested, I'll teach you how to thread the beads using a sewing needle if you think that might help."

To help your child develop the skill, persistence, and frustration tolerance inherent to many projects, work on some together as soon as he is old enough to contribute. For instance, team up with your child to plant a garden, build a birdhouse, assemble a toy, and so on.

Wean your support over time
Children need less and less support as they grow in experience, cognitive ability, emotional resilience, and physical strength. Since this growth can be slow, it's sometimes easy to get stuck giving your child the same level of assistance year after year. This is particularly true with tasks he considers unpleasant, like homework. The last thing your child wants is for you to pull the rug out from under him. In fact, he'd probably be as happy as a bee in a tulip farm if you were to do all his homework for him. So although your children will require homework support early on, wean them from your assistance as they get older. By the time they're in fourth or fifth grade, most of them need only occasional help. Once they're in middle school, they rarely need support. Be sure never to nag your child to do homework. She will become academically motivated only when you let the responsibility of her schoolwork fall on her shoulders and bear none of it yourself. Your role is to provide time, support when genuinely needed, and an environment conducive to studying and doing other homework.

Hold high but healthy expectations
When children are encouraged to do their personal best, they often rise to the occasion. Sometimes they just need a little parental input to figure out how high the bar can

be raised. So hold high expectations for your child, but be reasonable. Even better, encourage your child to have healthy expectations for his own performance. Express your expectations not as demands but as a loving message that you have faith in your child to reach his full potential and to accomplish anything he has his mind and heart set on.

Encourage hobbies and other skill-building activities
Hobbies and other activities tailored to children's interests offer a golden opportunity to build the skills necessary to become independent. So pay attention to the hobbies and other activities your child enjoys. Help her develop skills related to her interests, or find resources in the community that offer learning-enrichment activities she might enjoy.

Talk, talk, talk with your child
As long as it's lecture-free and captures their interest, dialogue between parent and child is an important tool for building independence. Converse with your child about issues big and small, from current events to what happened in each other's day. This not only helps develop conversational and listening skills, but it also imparts knowledge and shows that you value what your child has to say.

Expose your child to a world of knowledge
To become independent, self-propelled learners, children need to be aware of the vast amount of information at their fingertips. Many, however, aren't exposed to these resources, even those a few blocks away. So take your child to libraries, community centers, bookstores, and

museums. Find out if any of these hold children's events. Be sure to make it an exciting adventure rather than a boring *duty*. Through these outings, you'll not only gain an awareness of your child's interests, he'll get a chance to explore and develop new ones.

Encourage practice

There's truth to the adage "Practice makes perfect." When children repeat the same skill over and over, their mistakes become fewer and their proficiency greater. Encourage your child to practice, practice, and practice his skills. Does that mean honing your nagging skills to a razor edge? No. Simply offer the opportunity to practice and provide the time, space, and equipment your child needs.

Find ways to make the practice fun! I used to sing a goofy little song when my children practiced tying their shoes. (Although given my vocal talents, I'm wondering why they're not still wearing shoes with Velcro straps.) If they refuse to practice, the discipline techniques described in chapter 7 should work: "I see you haven't practiced piano today, and your teacher will be here within an hour. You asked to take up lessons. That's a commitment. And since Smiths honor their commitments, I suggest you start soon." Try giving a limited choice: "When would you like to practice piano, now or after supper?" Or leave it to the natural consequence that will surely befall him when his piano teacher hears him play!

Encourage challenges

When children take on a challenging task, the risk of mistakes or out-and-out failure is great. As we have learned, these setbacks are just stepping-stones to success. Given enough time hopping from one stepping-stone to the next, your child will develop a healthy attitude for failure. Furthermore, he will acquire a broad range of complex skills—something only challenge and struggle can provide. And the more difficult tasks he masters, the stronger his self-confidence will become. That said, invite your child to take on challenges, and not just those with a guarantee of success. Let her curiosity and enthusiasm lure her into situations that might end in failure. At a young age, the emotional investment children have in new endeavors usually isn't very high. So if they fall flat on their face, it won't devastate them. This is a good way for children to develop defeat-recovery skills.

Value the attempt
Even when children aren't successful at a task, there is a treasure chest full of valuable lessons hidden in their attempts. When your child fails, show him that you value him for trying: "I really admire the courage you showed trying out for the pole-vaulting team." Praising a child's attempts as well as his perseverance teaches that effort is more important than results. It's the journey, not the destination.

Remain objective
Nothing hampers a child's attempts to be independent more than a board of Olympic judges holding up scorecards. Children do better when they focus on what they're doing instead of how they're measuring up to others. They need objective feedback, not subjective evaluations. So never criticize or ridicule when your child struggles or fails in an emerging skill. Children need to

sense our faith in them to eventually succeed, and they need to know we'll love them even when they fail. Parents are not fair-weather friends. Our love is never defined by their successes or failures. It just is.

Point out newly acquired skills
Sometimes children have difficulty recognizing what they've gained from a task they've just attempted, especially if they were met with failure rather than success. So when your child fails, point out the skills he acquired in the process: "I know you may be disappointed about not getting that part in the school play, but just think — the tryout helped you overcome your shyness about speaking in public, and you seem more confident about your skills in debate class."

Start early and small
The earlier children march on that bumpy road to independence, the smoother their journey will be and the sooner they'll reach their destination. So let your child take on small feats as early as possible. As they get older, the challenges they accept should grow in complexity and required effort.

Give feedback
Sometimes children need to be reminded to look back on the ever-lengthening road behind them so that they can appreciate the fruits of their efforts and courage. When your child masters a skill that showcases her growing independence, give her that little tap on the shoulder through feedback based on your objective observations: "Last year you weren't able to button your coat on your

own, but just look at you now! You can handle so many things on you own. I guess you're really growing up."

Encourage a broad range of independence
To live successfully as adults, children need to develop independence in areas other than academic, physical, personal care, and practical life management. Help your child develop skills in planning, organization, decision-making, resistance, interpersonal areas (empathy, sensitivity, and establishing and maintaining friendships), conflict resolution, and problem-solving. Some of these we've already covered, while others we'll discuss later on.

Point out the benefits of independence
When children master a skill independently, some of the positive effects can reach beyond what is immediately obvious. Lest they go unnoticed, point out some of these overlooked but powerful benefits: "I bet you're glad you can tie your own shoes instead of waiting for me to do it for you. Your little sister is still a baby and can't do anything for herself. It must be hard to have to depend on someone for everything."

Encourage perseverance
We all know it's not easy to keep our nose to the grindstone when the task gets boring or when the failed attempts mount. Give positive feedback when your child demonstrates the perseverance that gaining independence often requires: "Look at you! You were just about to give up on learning to ride your new bike, but you hung in there and did it! Now you can ride bikes with your brother!"

Make "sincere" requests for help

Parents normally don't need their children's help, particularly when kids are very young. In fact, that "help" is usually anything but. However, the "pain" of watching your kid slowly, laboriously learn a new skill has a "gain"—a child whose growing proficiency will make your parenting job easier, more joyful, and less tedious the older he gets.

When you want your child to learn a new skill, present it as a sincere request for assistance rather than a requirement she must meet to gain experience, develop independence, and become responsible. Fake it if you must. For instance, if you say to your daughter, "I'm so swamped with breakfast dishes that I'm afraid I'll be late for work. I could really use your help. Would you mind bringing in the paper and feeding the dogs?" chances are she'll be eager to help and proud to be needed. But if you were to say instead, "Kristina, it's your turn to bring in the paper and feed the dogs. I don't want to have to remind you again. You need to take the initiative next time," she'll probably moan and groan, roll her eyes as if they were Cirque du Soleil acrobats in training, and eventually shuffle out the door, leaving knuckle drag marks along the way. To inspire even more eagerness in your child, tailor your request to the child's uniqueness:

> "Annika, my favorite pen rolled under the sofa. You're the only one with hands small enough to reach it. Could you give it a shot?"

> "I can't find my glasses anywhere. Michelle, you've always had such keen vision, and you're much better than I am at thinking up places to look. Could you

see if you can find them for me? I could really use your help."

Remarks like these give a child the message that she is valued and does have a meaningful and contributing role in the family. And to become heroes, children must feel valued.

Easing the transition from childhood to adulthood

The best way to prepare children for life in the adult world is to equip them with the skills they'll need as grown-ups. Even toddlers can begin to acquire skills that will help them as adults. As our children grow, we can tailor those skills to their level of development and maturity. Naturally, the required skills will become more complex and challenging as time goes on. Although every child is unique, here are some suggestions:

Nursery school—ages 18 months to 3 years
- Straighten bed upon awakening
- Put away pajamas
- Put dirty clothes in hamper
- Clear meal dishes that pose no chance of spill or breakage
- Brush hair with help
- Put books away
- Choose breakfast foods
- Undress self (ages 2 to 3)
- "Fold" and put away clothes
- Pick up toys

- "Set" the table with plastic dishes and napkins
- Wash small non-breakables in a basin with supervision
- Check on pet's well-being and inform you of pet's needs (e.g., food and water)
- Wash sticky toys with a damp rag
- Pet the pet daily so it knows it is loved
- Throw away dirty diapers
- Sweep the stoop with a child-sized or whisk broom
- Finish stirring batter, cleaning vegetables
- Match socks
- "Fold" washcloths and napkins
- Flush toilet
- Wash hands before meals and at bedtime
- Help parents with younger sibling by fetching diapers and toys

Preschool—ages 3 to 4

- Pick up room with intermittent supervision
- Feed or water pets
- Dust a piece of furniture with light polish
- Make a simple sandwich
- Wipe off counter and table
- Make a simple fruit salad (peel bananas and slice with a dull knife, section oranges, rinse and separate grapes)
- Tear lettuce
- Take out small garbage bags
- Sort recycling
- Cut coupons with safety scissors
- "Fold" towels
- Help shop and put away groceries

- Polish shoes
- Prepare cold cereal
- Make a simple dessert
- Help tend to the garden, with supervision (watering plants, weeding, sowing seeds, and so on)

Kindergarten — ages 5 to 6
- Prepare a small yard for mowing (pick up sticks and toys, move folding chairs to patio)
- Tend a small garden (planting, supervised weeding and watering, harvesting)
- Groom pets that are patient and shorthaired
- Run the vacuum (for familiarity, mostly) and eventually vacuum hallways
- Clean bathroom sink, tub, and toilet
- Bathe pets
- Put groceries away
- Sweep the walk
- Choose appropriate dress
- Bathe self (although some may not be able to rinse hair)
- Send thank-you drawings
- Take out garbage
- Make a simple lunch and breakfast
- Pour own drink
- Choose gifts for loved ones
- Continue cooking skills that do not involve heat and sharp knives
- Put toys away consistently
- Make bed and clean room
- Dress self and choose clothing
- Scrub sink

- Fold and put clothes away
- Set part or all of the table
- Clear dishes from the table

Elementary school—ages 6 to 9

- Learn higher cooking skills (use of sharp knives, closely supervised meal planning, nutrition, content, and so on)
- Begin intensive kitchen safety training
- Water plants
- Walk dog
- Train pets
- Get up in the morning and go to bed by themselves
- Take care of school supplies
- Carry their own money
- Clean the inside of the car
- Take care of minor injuries
- Peel vegetables
- Be polite and courteous
- Take simple phone messages
- Care for bike
- Wash walls and floors
- Clean blinds
- Run bath water
- Help others with their work
- Shop for and select their own clothing with a parent
- Change school clothes
- Write simple letters and thank-you notes
- Feed a baby
- Dust and wax furniture

- Manage own study/homework times with supervision
- Hang up clothes
- Learn about safe and proper use and dangers of cleaning supplies
- Set the table consistently
- Sweep floors
- Feed and water pets
- Load and unload the dryer
- Rinse dishes
- Take out garbage
- Unload the dishwasher of non-breakables that belong within reach
- Load the dishwasher of non-breakables
- Put food away after a meal
- Make lunch for school
- Lay clothes out the night before
- Keep room clean
- Help younger siblings get ready in the morning
- Help fold most of the laundry
- Understand the purpose of dialing 911

Elementary school—ages 9 to 11
- Keep room clean and organized
- Plan and prepare easy meals
- Clean one room other than own on a weekly basis
- Empty garbage
- Clean the garage or basement

By fifth grade
- Earn their own money
- Be alone at home
- Handle self properly alone or with friends
- Handle money up to $20 honestly

Middle school—ages 11 to 14

- Change sheets
- Do light mending
- Take complex phone messages and show proper phone etiquette
- Iron clothes
- Mow the lawn (ages 12 and up)
- Know what to do in a simple emergency
- Know how to do the Heimlich maneuver on a smaller child
- Schedule own study time
- Give directions
- Ask for directions
- Give proper change
- Bake cookies, pies, and cakes alone
- Use washer and dryer with little supervision
- Buy groceries from a list
- Prepare box recipes and more complex meals
- Wait on guests
- Plan own party
- Perform simple first aid
- Wash the car
- Do chores without reminding
- Wash windows
- Help with house painting

High school—ages 15 to 18

- Pick up siblings from school activities (when able to drive)
- Baby-sit until late night (overnight for 18-year-olds)
- Shop for own clothes
- Create and follow a budget

- Sort, pre-treat, wash, and dry laundry
- Handle all lawn maintenance (mowing, weed-eating, fertilizing, trimming trees and hedges, and so on)
- Paint a room
- Set and obtain long-term goals like earning money to buy a car
- Create a detailed life plan divided into short, intermediate, and long-term periods and follow it (see later in this chapter for how to help your child construct and manage life plans)
- Show character: integrity, responsibility, accountability, reliability, compassion, tolerance, and so on
- Consistently make responsible choices
- Manage the entire college-application process, including asking for letters of recommendation, choosing colleges, learning what courses are available, determining if the college fits career plans, filling out and mailing applications, writing college essays, scheduling interviews and orientations, preparing for admissions testing, exploring scholarship and financial-aid options, directing questions to the admissions office, and so on
- Help paint part or all of the house exterior (some 18-year-olds doing this by themselves)
- Go to a doctor's appointment alone
- Handle customer complaints well
- Handle fire, medical, and security emergencies in most cases
- Diaper, bathe, and care for an infant
- Take care of older relatives
- Prepare more difficult meals (at least once a month for high schoolers)

- Run errands
- Create a résumé or C.V.
- Fill out a job application
- Master interview techniques
- Schedule a job interview and handle it well
- Demonstrate sound work ethics
- Arrange for repairs on broken appliances and equipment
- Obtain technical support by phone
- Help someone move
- Help pay the family household bills (short of signing the checks) either manually or using a financial software such as Quicken
- Make appointments
- Grocery shop
- Clean and wash car, change oil, rotate tires
- Sew
- Prepare income-tax forms for self
- Acquire rudimentary investment knowledge
- Experiment with mock investments and follow them over time
- Balance checkbook and reconcile own bank statements, if they have their own bank account
- Establish and adhere to a sound savings plan divided into charitable giving, essential ongoing expenses, discretionary wants, and long-term goals

Naturally, the boundaries between these age groups are anything but distinct. After all, kids develop in different areas and at different rates. That said, let this list serve as a rough guide. It's better to encourage children beyond what we think they're capable of handling. Just be there while they first learn to answer questions, and ensure they're following safe practices. More often than not, they surprise us more than they surprise themselves.

Organizations that mentor and guide kids

Youth development programs are another way to equip your child with the skills he needs to thrive as an adult. Many programs are nationwide. Although each has its own unique focus and specialized activities, choose one that provides children with opportunities to

- Be responsible
- Belong to and be a valued member of a group
- Work cooperatively in groups, lead, and develop a sense of community
- Be heard—to discuss and reflect on ideas, express themselves through a variety of mediums, and practice a variety of communication skills
- Participate in engaging, diverse skill-building activities and make choices based on interest
- Engage in active learning
- Set goals with staff assistance
- Learn and practice new skills and talents
- Define standards of behavior
- Be involved in decision-making
- Assess and give feedback
- Plan, share plans, and implement activities
- Contribute, work, earn, and participate in community development.

The Web site for the Forum for Youth Investment (FYI) (*www.forumforyouthinvestment.org*) is the source of the preceding list of prerequisites. FYI is dedicated to improving the quality of youth programs through planning, research, advocacy, and policy development among organizations that invest in children, youth, and families.

FYI's Web site contains papers, articles, and editorials reporting research results and providing information on the design, management, and effectiveness of youth development programs. Browse through these, and subscribe to the informative *FYI Newsletter*.

Although this is by no means a complete list of my favorites, here are some programs worthy of consideration:

4-H Youth Development Program
(*www.fourthcouncil.edu*)
This is the site for the National 4-H Council, which can direct you to a local 4-H program. Not just limited to agricultural programs, 4-H also offers young people ways to take part in more than 110 areas, including

- Community service
- Communications
- Arts
- Consumer and family sciences
- Environmental education
- Earth sciences
- Healthy lifestyle education
- Leadership
- Plants and animals
- Science and technology

Because of its global coverage, exchange programs are also offered. You can subscribe to their newsletter,

Power of YOUth, sign up as a volunteer, and give donations through the Web site above.

The Rose Foundation (*www.rosefoundation.org*)

This international organization provides young people with programs that "promote and facilitate collegial behavior, creative expression, cooperative working skills, independence, and responsibility while empowering them to achieve their own desires and become active, constructive, caring members of the community."

Here are examples of programs offered:

- "Building Self-Esteem and Success": Covers issues of personal growth and development and ways kids can deal with peer pressure
- "Anger Management and Conflict Resolution as Learning Tools": Focuses on learning skills to defuse difficult situations; teaches communication and peer mediation as a process in resolving problems
- "Going Places, Making Changes": Designed to help kids understand and respond to real life issues, build partnerships with adults, explore career opportunities, and begin to acquire skills to build a successful future
- "Youth Scholars Leadership Institute Scholarship Program": An international mentor and exchange program that starting in 2005 will provide scholarship opportunities within home and host countries, allowing young people to broaden their educational horizons while securing career opportunities in their respective countries or with a sponsoring organization

Campfire USA (*www.campfireusa.org*)

This well-known organization offers coeducational programs to girls and boys to cultivate their unique talents and skills in small-group environments. Although youth-centered, Campfire engages the entire family in fun, outcome-rich activities. Individual accomplishments are recognized and rewarded within the group and community. Personal skill-building and decision-making are critical components of Campfire's program, which progressively builds confidence and leadership in its young members.

Girl Scouts of the USA (*www.girlscouts.org*)

Since 1912, the Girl Scout program has delivered quality experiences for girls locally, nationally, and internationally. Like Campfire, programs are conducted in a small-group environment. Program goals include developing self-potential, relating to others, developing values, and contributing to society. Driven by age-appropriate, incremental goals, Girl Scouts encourages increased skill-building and responsibility and promotes the development of strong leadership and decision-making skills.

Boy Scouts (*www.scouting.org*)

Similar to the Girl Scouts, this is a program that offers character, citizenship, and personal-fitness training for boys. Goal-driven programs foster a high degree of self-reliance by inspiring such qualities as initiative, courage, and resourcefulness; instilling personal values based on religious concepts; nurturing the desire and skills to help others; teaching the principles of the American social, economic, and governmental systems; imparting knowledge about and a sense of pride in the American heritage and an understanding of our nation's role in the world; developing a keen respect for the basic rights of all people; and becoming prepared to participate in and lead American society.

Community Impact! (*www.impactusa.org*)

This organization offers a teen financial-literacy program that trains urban fifteen- to twenty-four-year-olds to increase educational and economic opportunities for themselves, their peers, and their neighborhoods.

Outward Bound (*www.outwardbound.com*)

Outward Bound wilderness adventures emphasize personal growth through experience and challenge. Programs of varying lengths and in locations worldwide immerse participants in nature through mountaineering, rock climbing, kayaking, backpacking, and canoeing.

Whether your child struggles in his journey to heroism or not, if he is fortunate enough to enroll, he will have an opportunity to discover and expand his emotional, mental, and physical limits. Entitlement wanes; responsibility and self-esteem soar, giving him a new perspective on life in terms of what's important and what's not and what it takes to care for himself and others.

In all programs and course settings, students develop self-reliance, responsibility, teamwork, confidence, compassion, and environmental and community stewardship. The Voyageur Ascent Course is specially designed for struggling teens.

I believe our government would best protect our future if participation in programs like Outward Bound were mandatory for all kids ages fourteen to eighteen.

Two to four weeks in a government-run or -sponsored wilderness program might sound costly to the average taxpayer, but in the long run, raising a nation of heroes is cheaper than not doing so. And thanks to the generous support of others, Outward Bound offers financial aid and scholarships to those who would otherwise regard the opportunity for such an adventure as an idle wish.

Walkabout (*www.walkabout-treatment.com*)
If your child struggles with irresponsible choices, poor self-esteem, a bloated sense of entitlement, and family conflict, don't despair! Walkabout, named after the aboriginal rite of passage where young men and women become adults, will help her overcome obstacles that block her path to heroism. Walkabout's goal is treatment, not wilderness or survival skills. Its wilderness setting removes material and technological distractions, moving participants out of their "emotional comfort zone." Then counselors can help them replace negative emotional habits with positive ones. The approach is based on individualized treatment, outdoor experiences, peer interaction utilizing a positive peer culture, and teaching each family the skills to help support their child's growth.

Struggling Teens (*www.strugglingteens.com*)
This site, created by Lon Woodbury, offers a wealth of information and services for kids who struggle in their mission to become heroes. Woodbury is an educational consultant who has worked with schools and programs for struggling teens since 1984. He offers a nationwide referral service for parents of adolescents with behavioral and emotional problems, writes "Woodbury Reports" (an

education newsletter), and publishes a directory as part of the results of his research into which schools and programs of quality are available for the child who is making poor decisions.

Online financial-literacy programs
- NEFE Teen Resource Bureau (*www.ntrbonline.org*) is a personal-finance Web site for young adults. It covers the basics of money management and helps teens learn more about buying a car, paying for college, establishing their independence, and having cash for the weekends.
- YoungBiz (*youngbiz.com*) provides information to teenagers on business, investing, and entrepreneurship.
- Consumer Education for Teens (*www.wa.gov/ago/youth/default.html*), written for teens by teens, helps young consumers avoid rip-offs. Topics covered include music clubs, tattoos, health clubs, car buying and repair, credit cards, car stereos, scholarship scams, Internet scams, telemarketers, apartment renting, and return policies.
- The College Financial Aid and Planning Counselor (*www.college-funds.com*) offers free financial-aid planning tips to save thousands of dollars and hours of headaches.

Using other adult mentors

Many adults are eager and willing to help children grow up to have strong character, to become capable and confident, and to contribute something special to the world. These hidden treasures are in our schools, our businesses, our places of worship, and even in our own families. Our job, as parents, is to identify adults who can serve as role models, academic or otherwise, for our children.

An adult mentor can help your child explore and develop her talents, build skills important to a successful future, and reflect on her ideas, problems, values, and dreams.

Although many communities have mentorship programs, you can also organize a mentoring co-op in your neighborhood by swapping kids with your neighbors, weekly or monthly. Take the kids on outings, introduce them to new activities and learning experiences, or just "hang out" with them as a non-threatening, objective, caring adult willing to listen to their concerns and problems without judging or criticizing them.

The article "Building Effective Youth-Adult Partnerships," by Jane Norman, Program Manager for Youth Empowerment Initiatives, on the Advocates for Youth Web site (*www.advocatesforyouth.org*), describes the benefits to a child of an adult mentor:

- Feel physically and emotionally safe
- Build relationships with caring, connected adults
- Acquire knowledge and information
- Engage in meaningful and purposeful activities in ways that offer both continuity and variety

Norman claims that resiliency research has identified certain "protective factors" that distinguish children who overcome adversity or high-risk situations. Protective factors that kids can acquire through relationships with adult mentors include

- *Social competence*: responsiveness, flexibility, communication skills, empathy and caring, a sense of humor, and other pro-social behaviors
- *Problem-solving skills*: the ability to think abstractly, reflexively, and flexibly, and the ability to arrive at alternative solutions to cognitive and social problems
- *Autonomy*: a sense of identity plus an ability to act independently and to exert control over their environment
- *Sense of purpose and future*: healthy expectations and goals, an orientation toward success, motivation to achieve, educational aspirations, hopefulness, hardiness, and a sense of coherence

Norman also cites research that says mentoring provides children with opportunities to develop and/or strengthen their internal locus of control, or the "feeling of being able to have an impact on one's environment and on others." A strong internal locus of control is another protective factor characterizing resilient youth. Benefits of mentoring, however, are not limited to the child. Adult mentors also enjoy positive changes in their lives:

- Experiencing the competence and contributions of youth firsthand
- Finding an enhanced commitment and energy from working with youth
- Feeling more effective and confident in working with and relating to youth
- Understanding the needs and concerns of young people

- Gaining a stronger sense of connection to the community
- Reaching a broader spectrum of people
- Sharing knowledge, increasing creativity, and receiving ideas from different perspectives

What elements does it take to establish a sound and effective youth/adult mentorship? Norman mentions that it's important for us to

- Establish clear goals for each person's role and responsibilities within the relationship.
- Tailor the responsibilities to the child's abilities and willingness. Provide the skill-building necessary to encourage further development in areas such as leadership, communication, assertiveness, interviewing, and so on.
- Share decision-making power.
- Be aware of different communication styles. Some styles do not imply disrespect, disinterest, or different goals and expectations. If you don't understand what is being said, ask for clarification.
- Value each other's participation and value to the relationship.
- Allow the child more responsibility over time.
- Respect the fact that kids have other interests and priorities. Don't enlist them in an overwhelming number of obligations and commitments.

Mentors are a valuable, often unrecognized, resource for that bumpy transition from childhood to adulthood! A positive and caring relationship with even one adult mentor other than parents can make a profound difference in the life and future of every child.

Helping children create a life plan

Despite belonging to a generation many regard as particularly ambitious, kids rarely have a life plan. Many see college admission as the be-all and end-all but have little clue how to transform their ambitions into goals and then how to implement those goals into a reality.

For instance, a child may have ambitions to become a record producer, but he takes no steps to learn about the recording industry. He doesn't pursue internships, enroll in special courses, or research the career through books, Web searches, and interviews with industry professionals.

And another child may spend a great deal of effort deciding what college to attend and taking steps to prepare himself for admission, but he devotes little attention to researching whether that college has the appropriate courses for his career dreams. His parents aren't helping much. They spend little time talking with him about his ambitions. Furthermore, they seldom give him the resources, guidance, and opportunities he needs to explore his options, confirm his choice, and make plans for turning that dream into a reality.

This child may wind up taking courses that he hates, changing majors two to three times, and ultimately giving up, dropping out, and moving back home.

Regardless of how hard some kids try, they seem to be running in place with no idea where to go. High ambitions are meaningless without informed choices and clear life plans for reaching them. If we parents help our children plan for their futures, they can see that by making a life plan, they're more likely to "get a life."

What is a life plan?

A life plan is a comprehensive list of a child's goals, ambitions, desires, and wants that, because of its tangible rather than abstract form, can be reviewed, modified, and prioritized over time. It also provides steps through which dreams can be realized.

Can you imagine building a 4,500-square-foot, two-story home without an architectural plan? How can we expect our children to build a life that can withstand the winds of change and adversity without a detailed blueprint to follow? Unless children have a life plan, dreams are no more than idle wishes that become muddied or forgotten over time. Furthermore, when children design their own plan, it provides them with an excellent opportunity to reflect on their dreams and on life in general.

When your child is about nine or ten, encourage him to create a life plan. Modify it from time to time as needed. This plan should cover the following life areas, in a depth and scope appropriate to your child's age and maturity: career and finances, health and wellness, mental health and education, family and home, society and culture, and spirituality and ethics.

Within each category, have your child list his or her goals. Each goal should be specific, measurable, and realistic. They should also be attainable within a specified target date, whether exact or approximate.

Encourage your child to prioritize these categories and the goals within each according to his or her preferences, not yours. Then help your child list the steps necessary to reach each goal.

A sample life plan — grade school

As early as third grade, your child can create a simple life plan that includes basic elements in each category. Here's one an elementary-school child might create. Bear in mind that this is not necessarily complete.

Career and finances

1. When I grow up, I want to be a veterinarian. I've always loved animals. I'm not sure if I want to take care of just cats and dogs or farm animals like horses.
2. I'm going to meet with our vet and ask him some questions about what it takes to become a veterinarian and what it's like. I'll also ask if I can help out in his office for an hour or two a day so I can see what it's like.
3. I've also thought about being a zookeeper. This summer, I'll sign up for the "Young Zookeepers" camp at our city zoo so I can learn more about the career.
4. Right now, how much money I make in a career isn't that important to me.

Health and wellness

1. I'm going to have healthier after-school snacks from now on, like cheese and crackers, a peanut butter sandwich, or grapes (not the purple ones, because they're yucky).
2. I'll try to eat dessert only once or twice a week except when it's around my birthday.

3. I will eat meals that are balanced and good for me.
4. I will not complain about going to my doctor to get my shots.
5. I will try to exercise at least three times a week. I'm joining the swim team this summer, so that should help. Plus, I'm going to ask Mom and Dad to let me take horseback-riding lessons.
6. I'll take a bath every day and wash my hands before meals.
7. I'll brush and floss my teeth at least twice a day.

Mental health and education
1. I will do my homework right after my snack instead of waiting.
2. I will try to do my best, check my work, and write as neatly as I can.
3. I will get together with Sarah and Emma to study for tests.
4. I will try to calm myself down by thinking happy thoughts when I'm about to take a test.

Family and home
1. I will try to ask Mom and Dad about their lives more.
2. I will spend more time with them too, instead of staying in my room all the time.
3. I will do my chores without being asked.
4. I will offer to help out more around the house.
5. I will try to be nicer to my little brother and watch over him for a while every day so Mom can take a rest.
6. I'm going to keep my room neater by putting up my toys when I'm finished with them, putting my

dirty clothes in the hamper instead of on the floor, and dusting and vacuuming every Sunday.

7. I'll call my grandma once a week.

Society and culture

1. I'm going to invite my friends over to my house more often.
2. I want to try to make at least one new friend every couple of months.
3. I'll listen to my friends more.
4. I'll use good manners when I talk to grown-ups and kids, even that new kid, Everett, who keeps sticking his tongue out at me. One thing I'll try to do is say "Excuse me?" instead of "Huh?" when I can't understand someone and answer with "Yes?" instead of "Huh?" when someone calls out my name.
5. I won't let Tommy bully me anymore. I'm going to make a plan for handling him without getting my lights knocked out.
6. I will refuse to do things that aren't right when my friends try to get me to.
7. I won't be so bossy with Lauren.

Spirituality and ethics

1. I'm going to start telling the truth more.
2. I'll join the youth group at our church.
3. I'll tell myself to stop and think if what I'm about to do feels wrong.
4. I'm going to write a letter to one person a month, telling them how great they are and how thankful I am to know them. I'll start with my teacher.

5. I'll try to see the good in everyone, even when they're mean to me.
6. I'll try to do a random act of kindness once a week. I'll start a "Kindness Club" so my friends and I can do some of these together.

A sample life plan — middle school

As your child gets older, the basic framework in the grade-school life plan will remain the same but will increase in complexity and scope. When he starts middle school, he can begin to formulate a more comprehensive plan, with your guidance. By then, he's likely to have the cognitive ability for more complex organization, long-range planning, and analyzing abstracts like potential education and career scenarios. Here's a sample of a life plan a child in this age group might create:

Career and finances
1. Find and complete an apprenticeship at a broker-age firm this summer.
2. Interview a stockbroker to learn how I might become one and how it is to be in that business.
3. Start saving money to buy a car.

Health and wellness
1. Go out for the track team.
2. Investigate and possibly attend a summer track-and-field camp to improve my skills.
3. Run at least three times a week.
4. Eat balanced meals and healthy snacks.
5. Limit my television and video games to four hours a week from Monday through Friday and one or two hours on weekends.

6. Take a shower every day.
7. Wash my hands before meals.
8. Brush and floss my teeth at least twice a day.
9. Get at least nine hours of sleep a night.

Mental health and education
1. Shoot for all A's and B's on my report card.
2. Attend math and social-studies tutorials before every test and quiz.
3. Read every day.
4. Turn in my homework on time.
5. Form a study group to prepare for big tests.
6. Establish a "study buddy" I can call if I have any questions about my assignments.
7. Be better about clarifying what I need to do for projects and what I need to study for exams.
8. Take one hour out of each day to relax and reflect.
9. Write down my feelings in my journal.
10. Talk to my mom and dad if I have any problems.

Family and home
This would be much the same as the grade-school life plan, with more detailed, concrete plans at a higher level of responsibility.

Society and culture
Your child might expand this section to include plans for his cultural development, like watching the Travel Channel, Discovery Channel, or PBS; visiting various museums; exploring a variety of music and literature, and so on. He may wish to take an etiquette course. He might join or form clubs that broaden cultural horizons

by exploring the customs, cuisine, and characteristics of other countries.

Spirituality and ethics

In this section, your child should, with your help, list values and principles most important to her and come up with strategies that will help her adhere to them, even in challenging situations. This can be her personal Code of Ethics.

Your child can also add a "service to the community" plan by writing down various weekly and annual service projects with which she wants get involved. To help guide her choices, encourage her to write down different causes about which she feels passionate and assist her, if she needs it, in the research necessary to finding service opportunities that best match those causes.

A sample life plan—high school

In high school, a life plan should include goals and responsibilities that are complex, detailed, concrete, and adult. These goals should be divided into short-term (one year), intermediate-term (two to five years), and long-term (five to ten years). The plan might include these items:

- Look into and perhaps apply for SAT preparation courses.
- Practice SAT flash cards daily.
- Take practice SAT tests weekly.
- Schedule and complete career-aptitude testing at Rice University (junior year).
- Narrow career/major possibilities.
- Talk to high school career counselor (bring results of career-aptitude testing).

- Get letters of recommendation from employers, teachers, and counselors.
- Select ten different colleges offering majors in my area of interest and examine course list, qualifications of professors, extracurricular activities, financial aid, job opportunities, and so on.
- Attend College Night March 5.
- Take SAT I April 2.
- Take SAT II September 3.
- Visit three top college choices over winter break.
- Discuss college experiences with my friends a year ahead of me.
- Research scholarship and student-loan opportunities and apply for those meeting my needs and suiting my eligibility.
- Apply for summer job as lifeguard.
- Finish internship at KLTH radio station and obtain letter of recommendation.
- Create résumé and have Mom review it for typos.
- Investigate housing possibilities for college.
- Complete and mail college applications.
- Write and polish college-application essays.
- Save up $500 for first-semester dorm supplies—bed linens, toaster oven, small refrigerator, and so on.
- Refinance car at lower interest rate and tune up before move to college.
- Complete community-service requirements.
- Find part-time job second semester freshman year of college.
- Attend volleyball tryouts at the college August 12: ten days before start of classes.
- Send out graduation invitations.

- Investigate service opportunities in the area surrounding the university.
- Record new e-mail addresses, regular addresses, and phone numbers of my fellow graduates.

Life plans should never be rigid. Review them with your child on a regular basis and help him make changes, celebrate his accomplishments, and build on his increasingly independent path.

More ways to guide kids into adulthood

Here are some other ways you can help to guide your child's transition to adulthood:

- When your child is old enough to understand, use every opportunity to express your faith in him to accomplish his dreams. Our kids must know that we believe in them. When I was around six years old, my mother grabbed me by the shoulders, looked me in the face, and said, "Elisa, you're going to go far in life." Although I still have a ways to go, that one remark inspired me to look inside myself to see what I had to offer and to transform that into personal success.
- To gain the confidence they need to realize their goals, children should be aware of those qualities that make them special. When you tuck your child in at night, make a habit to list some of the unique and positive traits you've observed in him, and let him know how grateful you are to have someone so special in your life. Other times, ask your child to tell you what strengths he thinks he has.

- Encourage your child (at any age) to explore her talents, strengths, and interests by taking her to bookstores and libraries where she can find more information. Enroll her in learning-enrichment activities so she can start to develop skills related to her interests.
- Find out about early-talent-identification programs so that, as soon as preschool, your child can receive an education that challenges him.
- As mentioned before, enlist the help of mentors within the family or community to help your child identify and develop her talents.
- As your child gets older, have her make three lists: one for her strengths and talents, one for her interests (career or otherwise), and one for her priorities in life.
- Help your child understand his personality style, learning style, and various aptitudes. Public universities and community colleges offer free or low-cost testing in these areas. Online, the widely used Myers-Briggs Type Indicator personality test is available at *www.personalitypage.com*. It's also offered at many community colleges for a nominal fee. This test determines four variables in one's personality. First is the introversion and extroversion variable. Second is the "sensing" (gathering information in a concrete or literal way) and "intuitive" (generating abstract possibilities from information gathered) variable. Third is the "thinking" (decisions made using logic and reasoning) and "feeling" (decisions made on what feels right) variable. Last are the "judging" and "perceiving" variables. Folks in the

judging category sometimes insist their space remain neat, orderly, and established. They also like closure, which means they feel best when things are settled. People in the perceiving camp want their space to be flexible, open-ended, and spontaneous. There are sixteen different combinations of these four variables, each of which provides deep insight into a one's personality. Corporations and some of the armed services rely on this test to help them place people in roles most suited to their personality. Having your child take the test as early as middle school is a wonderful way for him to understand his innate personality strengths and how they can best be tapped, to be wary of his personality weaknesses, and to understand why he gets along well with some people and not others. Many schools, educational diagnosticians, Web sites, and other resources can help determine whether your child learns best by sight (visual learner), by sound (auditory learner), by movement (kinesthetic learner), or any combination of the three (multi-sensory learner). Knowing how your child learns best not only enables her to study more effectively, but it also gives her another clue toward figuring out what careers suit her best. Once a child does have an idea of a career or life path, aptitude tests can sometimes confirm her choice or give alternatives she hasn't considered. I recommend that children undergo career-aptitude testing in their junior year of high school. Many universities and community colleges offer this service for a reasonable fee.

- Persuade your child's middle school and high school to include life planning in the curriculum. In fact, I encourage all parents to join forces advocating courses in life planning and transitioning to adulthood as a graduation requirement. Casting your high school graduate into the world without well-defined goals, a strong life plan, or a clear idea about what the future holds for him is like tossing your kindergartner out the front door and telling him to do the family grocery shopping. If by some stroke of luck he makes it there and back, he's probably bringing home a grocery bag full of Snickers bars.
- When your child is in high school, encourage her to seek internships or volunteer opportunities to help explore her career plans. Encourage your child's school to establish work and internship programs with local businesses and institutions.
- To help your teen plan for his future, encourage him to save money for a special purpose, and teach him how to go about finding a summer job.
- Supervise and guide your adolescent in the college-application process with open-ended questions and feedback that will inspire him to ask himself:

> "To whom can I talk so I can make sure this college is right for me?"
>
> "To whom can I talk in the industry to make sure I want to follow this career?"
>
> "What internships are available to help me explore this career?"

"What are other ways I can get more experience?"

"Does this college have the courses I need and like?"

"What are the entrance requirements?"

"What are the living-arrangement options?"

"What scholarships, loans, or other financial aid does it offer?"

"How accessible are the professors?"

"Does it have mentoring programs on campus?"

"Does it have alliances with the industry where I want to build my career? Do those alliances include job-placement assistance, mentor relationships, work programs, or other opportunities and resources?"

"How long is the educational process for this career? Am I truly willing to go through it?"

"How are my interests and talents utilized in this career?"

"What else do I need in the way of steps or resources to successfully meet my career-planning goals?"

More questions will undoubtedly come to mind, but it's important to stick with your role as your child's guide by supervising the process rather than reverting to being the manager and taking over. Your job is to make sure your child makes informed choices, not to make the choices for him.

- Arrange for college visits and accompany your adolescent to ensure she gets all the information she'll need to make an informed decision.
- Visit *www.collegeboard.com* with your child so that, together, you can learn about the college-admissions process. The site offers your college-bound student a personal online organizer tailored to this often complex and laborious process. It also provides assistance in choosing and exploring a variety of careers.

When you help your child prepare himself for success in the adult world, his spirits are never in danger of being broken by reality's heavy hand. Fewer surprises, fewer uncertainties—these all make that transition from childhood to adulthood a smooth and fulfilling one. And without the obstacles these uncertainties create, your child can go about the business of living a hero's life.

Helping children find ways to contribute to their world

There's nothing children want more than to feel valued. Unfortunately, many times they don't. Why? Because they're seldom given opportunities to have meaningful, contributing roles in society. But they really do like to contribute, to help, to be an important and necessary part of society. When given the opportunity, their self-esteems soar, they acquire more skills, they see others and life in a more positive light, they feel more compassion and empathy toward others, they build a strong sense of self, they develop self-respect, and they feel—and are—empowered. Feeling valued is perhaps the most powerful ingredient in raising heroes—and after all, if heroes aren't to be valued, who is?

As I discussed in chapters 8 and 10, you can create opportunities for your child to contribute, both as a family and an individual, either within or outside the family. Also encourage contribution on a broader and larger scale, particularly when a child is older. Here are some possibilities:

- Encourage even your smaller children to make gifts rather than buy them.
- Older children can join service organization such as these:
  - Youth Service America (*www.ysa.org*) is a resource center and premier alliance of over three hundred organizations committed to increasing the quantity and quality of service opportunities for youth. It's a great avenue for finding project ideas or existing projects in which to participate. Details for National Youth Service Day, held every April, are found on this Web site.
  - Americorps (*www.americorps.org*) is a network of national service programs that engages more than 50,000 Americans each year in intensive service to meet needs in education, public safety, health, and the environment. AmeriCorps members serve through more than 2,100 non-profits, public agencies, and faith-based organizations. They tutor and mentor youth, build

affordable housing, teach computer skills, clean parks and streams, run after-school programs, and help communities respond to disasters.

- Habitat for Humanity (*www.habitat.org*) is a nonprofit, nondenominational Christian organization that provides a great opportunity for physical service. In communities across the nation and globally, volunteers help build decent, affordable housing.

- Students Against Destructive Decisions (*www.saddonline.com*) is an organization that involves, using their own description, "Students helping students make positive decisions about challenges in their everyday life." It's a peer-leadership organization dedicated to preventing destructive decisions like underage drinking, drug use, teen depression, and suicide. Your child can join an existing chapter or start a new one.

- Kids for Saving the Earth (*www.kidsforsavingearth .org*) is an organization founded by an eleven-year-old victim of cancer, now deceased, who was concerned by what we are doing to our planet. It's devoted to inspiring, informing, and empowering children to protect the future of our environment. Information and activities are offered to six different age groups from three through adult.

- Youth Activism Project (*www.youthactivism.com*) is an organization that gives young people a voice and an opportunity to play a major role in the causes that impassion them. Kids can explore the "Youth Action Line" for guidance in choosing a cause, joining an existing service organization or starting their own, finding ways to publicize their efforts, and figuring out how to reach community leaders who can help them further that cause. It also offers tips for success and a list of organizations that kids can consult to improve those chances. The Web site is a national clearinghouse of assistance and information for parents, teachers, mentors, principals, policymakers, and other adult allies.

- Church-based or -sponsored organizations.

- Children can help plan neighborhood gatherings, including service-related ones. Our street of seven houses has adopted an annual service tradition. One spring, we all pitched in our time, sweat, and (debatable) know-how to build an entire house for a Habitat for Humanity family. Each child was given tasks that were age-appropriate. Even smaller projects can have a positive impact on your child. For instance, you can encourage them to pick up litter on the sidewalk instead of passing it by. If she balks because she isn't the guilty party, respond with something like, "I know you didn't do it, but our neighborhood is our responsibility, and your help is very important to making it a good place to live." Other examples include holding a neighborhood book drive so that your child, along with the rest of your neighbors, can donate old books to the neighborhood library, cleaning up the neighborhood park as a group, collecting old toys and clothes and donating them to a shelter for women and children or another charity, and so on.

- Encourage your children to write anonymous letters of gratitude to teachers, police officers, firemen, neighbors, friends, and anyone else who is an important part of their lives. This helps children feel the power that unconditional and genuine kindness has, not only for the welfare of others but for theirs as well.
- With your children, help a neighbor by shoveling snow from their driveway, bringing them food, taking in their paper and mail, taking care of their pets, doing some household cleaning when they're sick, and so on.
- Encourage your children to adopt service activities that relate to their strengths and interests.
- Help them explore the nature, consequences, and benefits of contribution by engaging in dialogue prompted by your open-ended questions.
- Use open-ended questions to help them understand that contribution is healthier than conformity as a means of gaining pack/group acceptance and that earning something is always preferable to taking or begging for it.
- Help your children take part in National Youth Service Day, the third Tuesday of April, when Youth Service America celebrates and recognizes the millions of hours our nation's youth has devoted to service for the year.
- Help them plan an activity for Make a Difference Day, dedicated to honoring neighbors helping neighbors. Created by *USA Weekend* and the Points of Light Foundation, Make a Difference Day is held on the fourth Saturday of October.

- Encourage your children to help younger siblings and then point out the powerful, positive effects of their kindness on both sides.
- Create a tradition where everyone in the family performs a daily random act of kindness and discusses it over dinner.
- Challenge your children to put their inhibitions aside to comfort someone who needs it.
- Work with your neighbors to instill a work/service ethic in each other's kids. Offer small jobs to each other's children. When we go on vacation, two neighbor kids feed and bathe my three dogs. They are eager to help, because they adore the dogs and feel proud that they could actually contribute something valuable to an adult! The same holds true for non-service-related jobs. All children must learn what it takes to earn money using their own sweat, ingenuity, and elbow grease. You'd be surprised by the creative entrepreneurial schemes children can invent. My nine-year-old son started a laminating and copying service for the neighborhood. Sadly, the cost of the laminating sheets and color ink were more than the price he charged for his services, but the price of not instilling him with a healthy desire to contribute through work would have been more costly.
- Encourage your child's schools to offer activities that help kids recognize their potential to become important contributors. Each student could be asked to identify something in the community he'd like to change. The next step is to develop and implement a plan to make that change.

Because all children are such treasures, this list could justify "Raising Everyday Heroes, Volume II." For now, I'll give you the short version in these last three sentences: It only takes our love, our guidance, and our encouragement to help our children carve out their own special niche in the realm of contribution and service. It is the nature of all heroes to leave this world a better place than when they came. And our children are up to that noble task.

11

Beyond the Family: How Society Can Pitch In

There are no problems we cannot solve together, and very few that we can solve by ourselves.

—Lyndon Baines Johnson

As our children's parents, we are primarily responsible to raise them to become ethical, self-confident, independent, and contributing adults. But we can always invite help, build allies, and tap other resources that will better their chances.

By taking our efforts beyond the white picket fence, we stir others to bring a new form of heroism to the world. If we limit our reach to our own children, we won't do them or ourselves any favors, because no matter how heroic they are, they'll be adversely affected by those who aren't. We parents need to do all we can to rally the larger community behind our hero-raising efforts. Our very future may depend on it.

Working with schools

Many educators are blessed with the gift of recognizing and bringing out the hero in every child. Some, of course, are not. Nonetheless, we need to build a positive, rather than a contentious, relationship with our children's teachers to form a team of advocates committed to raising a world of heroes. Some of the suggestions that follow may have already been incorporated by your child's school, while others may take time to implement. After all, teachers today are inundated with challenging requirements from many sources. Your job is to plant seeds diplomatically and compassionately while acknowledging the stresses teachers already have; to present these suggestions as a practical plan with specific, doable steps; and to alleviate some of the burden on teachers by helping implement and maintain your suggestions.

Here are ways you can work with your schools to encourage heroism in every grade:

- Build harmonious relationships with school personnel: teachers, administrators, and ancillary employees. Disagreements should be handled constructively, with respect and understanding. One way to develop healthy relationships is to be an active participant at school whenever you can. Although difficult for working parents, volunteering in the classroom, either occasionally or regularly, gives you a unique opportunity to observe your child's social and academic skills, how she fits in with her peers, and what external pressures and influences are prevalent on campus. The more information you have, the better equipped you'll be to guide your child.

- Acknowledge the challenges that teachers face, such as low pay, long hours, diminishing autonomy, budget cuts, demands from parents and administrators, as well as state and federal regulations for testing, curricular content, special needs, and diversity tolerance. They need words of encouragement and admiration.

- Be involved in your child's school by joining committees that interest you, participating in the PTA, reading to a child, or simply running photocopies or shelving books. Any contribution, large or small, creates community.

- Encourage your school to form partnerships with community organizations to open avenues through which students can volunteer, acquire skills, and establish mentoring relationships with other adults.

- Appeal to your school to encourage community service if it doesn't already do so.
- Talk to your school's curriculum team about whether self-direction skills and character-building can be part of an integrated curriculum. For instance, students can read literature that deals with these topics and then use it as a springboard to develop skills in analytical writing, critical thinking, grammar, and so on. An excellent source of this type of literature is *Books That Build Character: A Guide to Teaching Your Child Moral Values through Stories*, by William Kilpatrick and Gregory and Suzanne M. Wolfe.
- Encourage your school to create leadership roles for students on the school board or in other decision-making committees—not as official seat-warmers but as individuals involved in making real choices.
- Schools should encourage more than academic and athletic achievement. As a parent, provide ideas for your school to celebrate community contribution and character, too. As history has shown, sometimes people with the poorest academic performance have contributed the most to society.
- Encourage your school to train older students to mentor, assist, and befriend younger ones. They can take turns as conflict mediators in the cafeteria and on the playground to help younger children develop peacemaking skills.
- If needed, persuade your school to relate to students in a way that builds heroism: using helpful forms of praise; discouraging rescuing or approval-seeking; nurturing a strong but realistic sense of

self; building problem-solving and critical-thinking skills; and so on. Donate a copy or two of this book to the school library—or rather than the usual holiday gift of paperweights or candles, give copies to your children's teachers.

- Help your school build cooperation skills in children by encouraging them to adopt the cooperative-learning model where students learn as a team through a variety of projects. The typical classroom using this model might arrange desks in groups of four, facing toward one another, rather than lining them all up in forward-facing rows as in the didactic-learning model most of us have probably experienced growing up.

- Advocate a curriculum that gives students the opportunity to recognize their unique strengths and talents and put them to use.

- Resist the urge to rescue your child from consequences received in school. Even when the consequences seem unfair, children can generally deal with them on their own. Furthermore, it gives them the opportunity to experience the reality that justice is not a given in the real world. However, when an unjust consequence is potentially damaging and well beyond the child's ability to handle, then it's OK to intervene if not doing so would be unacceptably and irreversibly harmful to him or others. But do so constructively and calmly instead of barreling into the school like a mother bear whose cubs have been threatened.

- Encourage your school to give our children the opportunity to contribute in the classroom by straightening up the room or assisting with tasks like copying papers, sorting, cutting, replenishing supplies, delivering memos to the main office, and so on.

This is by no means a complete list. Every school differs in methods and attitudes, and as parents, we can use our own creative genius to cultivate other ideas. By combining our ideas, talents, passions, love of children, and dedication to their well-being with others who feel the same, we can work together to build a powerful and effective school/parent partnership that can bring out the hero in all children.

Working with the community

Alliances with various communities can provide enormous resources, support, and opportunities to further our mission to raise heroes. If you already have such alliances and are well-connected with business or political leaders, you have the power to bring about bigger changes over a shorter period of time than many. Although those who aren't blessed with such connections can also help create community hero-raising, the suggestions at the end of this chapter will apply more to those who have their own ten-person staff complete with executive assistant, secretaries, butlers, and lackeys or who already have strong bonds with the movers and shakers that can implement programs and changes.

Here are a few suggestions for establishing partnerships and putting them to constructive use:

- Get involved in town politics to help create meaningful roles for kids. For instance, you can present ideas at city council meetings for peer-to-peer mentoring programs, youth "service to the community" days, internship programs with local businesses, and so on. Assess your own community for specific needs, formulate a detailed plan, garner support from friends and neighbors, and jointly present your plan at the meeting. You can also use your involvement in town politics in other ways. For instance, you can encourage community leaders to create opportunities for young people to have a voice in policy-making and other community-related decisions. Perhaps some of the community board meetings can invite teen representation. Younger children can be invited to observe the proceedings as eager audience members.

- Challenge the stereotypes of youth by applauding their contributions in the community either in your conversations with others or in your statements to committees, councils, and other groups of community leaders. And when you witness good citizenship, character, and contributions from kids in the community, let them know personally how much they are appreciated.

- Attend community events as a family to keep abreast of the community's pulse and to establish yourself as an important part of a cohesive network. Examples include fun runs, county fairs, concerts in the park, Independence Day bicycle parades, community picnics, and so on.

- Encourage kids to get involved in community events, organizations, and businesses so that others can appreciate their potential as heroes and so that they also feel like an important part of the whole. For those younger than seventeen or eighteen (and sometimes even for them), back your encouragement with whatever assistance your child needs to make his involvement materialize from dream to reality. For instance, you might need to call various agencies to research opportunities for youth involvement and schedule a time for your child to volunteer.

- Help find sponsoring partners for special events within the community such as Career Day, Youth Service Day, and so on. You can devote your involvement to existing events, or if you have the talent and the passion, you can organize new ones.
- Get involved with or help run community-sponsored youth-support groups that help impart hero-building skills like peer resistance, social competence, conflict resolution, life planning, transition to adulthood, the college-application process and coping with the stress it creates, and so on. Some communities may already have groups that provide these benefits, such as the YMCA, Boys and Girls Club, Big Sister/Big Brother, or youth ministries from local churches. These groups are always eager to have adult volunteers. Those of you that are particularly ambitious or well-connected can help organize new support groups.
- If you'd like to start your own youth support group in the community, turn to the Youth Activism Project, mentioned in chapter 10. The project's founder and nationally recognized expert Wendy Lesko has

written a valuable resource titled *Maximum Youth Involvement: The Complete Gameplan for Community Action.* In it, she answers one hundred questions that cover every kind of challenge and situation. She also compares various models to figure out what level of youth involvement makes sense for you and identifies essential organizational supports. In addition, its step-by-step advocacy skill-building activities and strategies help adults as well as young people adapt to new roles. The forty-page appendix is a gold mine for in-house training sessions for staff, adult coordinators, community coalitions, and so on, as well as youth conferences and summits. Reproducible checklists and handouts will save you hours in preparation. To give you an idea of how this manual can help you organize a youth support group in your community, here's a small sample of the questions it answers:

How can youth infusion be introduced to an organization or coalition?

What organizational commitment and funding is necessary?

What are various staffing arrangements to consider?

What outcomes should be evaluated?

What are some initial recruiting strategies?

How should we approach schools?

What are some community checkpoints?

What strategies reduce youth turnover?

What activities help bridge the generation gap?

How do we secure necessary funding?

What are some youth-oriented publicity strategies?

You can order a copy through *www.youthactivism*
.com or by phone, 1-800-KID-POWER.

- Start a local chapter for those youth-related national organizations that aren't represented in your community. The parent organization will be happy to provide step-by-step guidance.

- If you own your own business or are responsible for hiring others, hire young people when possible and mentor them in gaining job skills. You can also offer times when your employees' children or those from the local area can spend a week watching, learning, and helping you out at work. Discuss this idea with your child's school to establish a good network of referral between other families and your business.

- Support youth-development programs like those described in chapter 10, either by making a dona-tion, volunteering in their behalf, or participating in their events.

- Join mentoring programs that give adults in the community the opportunity to mentor and guide youth. Some communities have mentor/youth pro-grams between the elderly in nursing homes or assisted-living establishments and kids from the surrounding neighborhood.

- If you're one of the lucky who are well-connected to business owners or community leaders, you can
  - Invite those in your business network to establish or sponsor mentoring partnerships, internships, after-school youth programs, community-service opportunities, and school-to-work programs for young people. An example: You could schedule a meeting with the CEO of your company to present a program where employees can reach out as mentors to area youth through either schools or youth groups in the community (like Boy Scout troops, Girl Scout troops, the local YMCA, and so on). Be sure to stress the benefits to the company from the public-relations stand-point and from being a part of a community whose young people grow to become responsible citizens and good role models for everyone. Rally the interest of other employees willing to help organize, publicize, and implement your plan. Other programs that rely on a business-community liaison include joint service projects (e.g., company-sponsored "Beach Clean Up Day"); summer internship programs and after-school work programs in conjunction with local high schools; and company-hosted workshops during assemblies or after school for peer resistance, conflict mediation, communication skills, job-application and -readiness training, and so on.
  - Convince community businesses to alter hiring practices so that preference is given to kids who have undergone an internship program,

completed a life-planning and -transition course, or demonstrated a strong devotion to service within the community.

- Encourage the decision-makers in your company to establish employee-incentive programs for involvement in youth-empowerment efforts. For instance, it would be fairly easy to create employee/youth mentorship programs either at the community center, churches, or schools. Employees could be invited to teach courses in career planning, financial literacy, work ethics, interview techniques, résumé development, assessing employee-benefit options, successful employee/management relations, customer-relations skills, leadership skills, team coopera-tion skills, and so on. If you work for or have ties with a local college or university, offer to help them organize an outreach program that gives seminars, workshops, or camps designed to build various skills in area youth to help them flourish as adults: leadership, communication, job interviewing, assertiveness, conflict resolu-tion, and so on. You can also help them estab-lish and run a mentoring program between college students and kids in the surrounding community.

When we succeed in building positive and construc-tive community partnerships committed to bringing out the best in every child, stereotypes will be shattered and barriers knocked down. The benefits to raising heroes will extend beyond child and family by gracing our communities with kids we can respect—kids who, as adults, will raise the bar for everyone.

Working with the media and other outside influences

Distracting and often harmful media messages are pelting away at our children's freshly minted resolve like hail on a tin roof. Children on their way to becoming self-directed heroes will eventually be skilled in filtering the external in a conscious and discriminating way. Until then, they remain vulnerable to harmful messages regardless of what we do to shelter them from that hailstorm.

There are ways, fortunately, of providing safe harbor along their journey so that their focus remains on strengthening and learning to use their own inner compass instead of diverting it to temptations that could lead them astray. As individuals, we can't very well beat a path to the corporate headquarters of *Allure* magazine, Proctor & Gamble, or CBS demanding that they present their messages in a fair, unbiased manner, untainted by greed or bottom lines. But we can act on a local level to support organizations dedicated to making sure our voices are not only heard but also counted. Such organizations help join us together so that, as a collective, we can convince the media industry to act in a socially responsible way. Here are some suggestions:

- Support and participate in community or school-based programs that help children develop resistance skills.
- Educate yourself. Before you can become an effective activist for responsible media, you must learn

how media impacts children and what recourse is available. Here are some resources:

- Media Channel (*www.mediachannel.org*) connects hundreds of affiliate organizations and sites involved in media concerns globally. Their motto is "As the Media Watch the World, We Watch the Media."

- Media Scope (*www.mediascope.org*) offers briefs and reports on the media's impact.

- Center for Media Education (*www.cme.org*) generates research and informational materials on "the potential—and the peril—for children and youth of the rapidly evolving digital media age."

- About Face (*www.about-face.org*) focuses on the impact mass media has on the physical, mental, and emotional well-being of women and girls.

- Families Interested in Responsible Media (FIRM) (*www.commonsensemedia.org*), offers a wealth of statistics, articles, and suggestions.

- The Center for Media and Public Affairs (*www.cmpa.com*) is a nonpartisan research organization that monitors trends and issues in media coverage.

- The Web site of the American Academy of Pediatrics (*www.aap.org/advocacy/mediamatters.htm*) presents a record of its testimonies before Congress about the impact of media on youth and offers reports and other resources on media-literacy issues.

- Other leading media and child-policy experts such as the Children's Partnership (*www.childrenspartnership.org*), Children Now (*www.childrennow.org*), the UCLA Center for Communication Policy (*www.ccp.ucla.edu*), the Kaiser Foundation (*www.kff.org*), and the Center for Media Education (*www.media-awareness.ca*) are worth investigating.
- A wonderful book that thoroughly addresses the media's effect on children is *The Other Parent*, by Jim Steyer.

- Boycott media and products that send unhealthy messages. If you think Revlon makes unfair promises for a wrinkle-free life, don't buy its products. Here are some organizations that are in your corner:
  - Co-op America (*www.coopamerica.org*) can offer a great deal of assistance here with its *Boycott Action News*, media– and human rights–related ratings for hundreds of companies, and so on.
  - Adbusters (*www.adbusters.org*) not only offers a magazine brimming with informative articles on the topic, but it also has a section called "Action Ideas" that gives suggestions on how to make your voice heard and offers an online store where you can buy posters to plaster throughout your town, school, or office. You have to see them for yourself, because they're difficult to describe in print. Suffice it to say that their hilarious yet powerful messages effectively express our collective demand for responsible media.

- ■ Commercial Alert (*www.commercialalert.org*) offers a moderated e-mail list to help families, parents, children, and communities defend themselves against harmful, immoral, or intrusive advertising and marketing and the excesses of commercialism.
- Support responsible programming by subscribing and donating to media companies that are creative, educational, unbiased, nonviolent, and diverse as well as those that invite active audience participation and critical thinking.
- If you have connections with those in your company who make marketing and advertising decisions, convince them to sponsor media that is socially responsible. Bob Wehling, recently retired chief marketing officer for Proctor & Gamble, and his colleague, Andrea Alstrup, senior vice president of advertising at Johnson & Johnson, developed the Family Friendly Programming Forum. Through it, they encouraged leading American advertisers to sponsor only those television programs that parents and children could enjoy together. Some of the companies that signed on include Coca-Cola, FedEx, AT&T, PepsiCo, McDonald's, and Kraft Nabisco. These companies alone represent $11 billion spent on television commercials every year. In other words, if advertisers take the initiative and encourage the media industry to do a better job, the hailstorm of harmful messages bombarding our children will abate dramatically. For media conglomerates, nothing speaks louder than cash hemorrhaging from their balance sheet.

- Write and submit movie reviews to help other parents choose wisely for their own children. One avenue through which to do this is Parents Reviewing the Media (*www.media-awareness.ca/eng/review.htm*).

- Petition, petition, petition! Petitions are one resource we, as individuals, can use to make ourselves heard. You can either sign an existing petition created by organizations advocating responsible media or create your own either manually or through *www.PetitionOnline.com*. Petition whom, you ask? For one, you can petition corporations to withdraw their advertising business from media that send harmful messages. Print, television, and radio media must, by law, donate a certain amount of time and exposure to broadcasting public-interest information. So why not fulfill that obligation promoting media-literacy programs, media-awareness campaigns, and so on? Additionally, you could petition Congress to increase funding for responsible programming. For instance, preferential funding could be provided for media not supported by corporate sponsors so that they can continue to develop and air programs or disseminate information in a socially responsible way. Grants to media-conglomerate giants like TBS or CBS might enable them to create responsible programming without relying on corporate sponsors whose advertisements are misleading or who are only willing to support sensationalistic programs that send children harmful messages. Last, you can petition these same media giants to set aside part of their profits to create and fund educational uses for the Internet.

- Form media/parent advocacy groups through local schools or churches to combine efforts that bring about and enforce changes in media which encourage responsible, creative, and selective thought in our children.

- Research and present various media-literacy curricula to your child's school or the school board, and encourage them to include media literacy in the curriculum as early as possible. By the time students are in second or third grade, they've already been inundated with harmful messages. A media-literacy program helps students develop the ability to access, analyze, evaluate, and process messages they're receiving. To be successful, it should accomplish these goals:

  1. Students will learn to use television, music, and other media in a responsible and discriminating manner.
  2. Students will learn to apply critical-thinking skills to analyze media messages and images.
  3. Students will learn to distinguish messages that represent propaganda from those that do not.

If this seems too overwhelming or time-consuming right now, support organizations devoted to the development and dissemination of media-literacy curricula. Here are some sources worthy of your attention:

  - Media Awareness Network (*www.education -medias.ca*) is an organization that is home to one of the most comprehensive collections of resources for media education and Internet literacy.

- Just Think Foundation (*www.justthink.org*) is an organization dedicated to teaching young people how to understand the words and images of today's media and to think for themselves. In 1998, it published its own media-literacy curriculum, *Changing the World through Media Education: A New Media Education Curriculum*. Later, it developed a ten-week curriculum aimed at fourth through twelfth graders entitled *Developing Minds* that includes a comic-style book for students, classroom materials on CD-ROM, and manuals for educators and parents. Just Think also offers outreach programs for teens as well as programs for curricular and staff development.

- Media Awareness Network (*www.media -awareness.ca/eng/default.htm*) is a Canadian Web site that offers practical support for media education in the home, school, and community. It is a world leader in providing educational approaches to emerging Internet-related issues and is committed to maximizing the positive aspects of all media for the benefit of our youth.

- Media Literacy Project (*www.reneehobbs.org*) offers a basic media-literacy curriculum, *Media Literacy*, as well as CD-ROMS and videos on the subject.

- Media Channel (*www.mediachannel.org*) is a nonprofit public-interest "supersite" dedicated to a range of media issues, including the

suppression of information by media conglom-
erates. It provides links to lesson plans, articles
by leading media-literacy scholars and activists,
and debates over such issues as media violence.
It also boasts a new education center for K–12
teachers, including teaching units, lesson plans,
handouts, and other tools from teachers and
media experts around the world.

- *Mediastudies.com* helps advance research and
education in media studies and critical thinking
by serving as a hub to educational guidelines,
global news outlets, and other resources for
media-literacy educators.

- Alliance for a Media Literate America
(*www.amlainfo.org*) was created at the 2001
National Media Education Conference to
enhance nationwide collaboration and "advocate for media literacy in ways that are more
powerful and influential than any individual,
project, or institution can achieve alone." Its
Web site emphasizes the importance of "critical
inquiry" and "skill building" rather than "media
bashing and blame." It also boasts a referral
service to connect media literacy specialists with
schools and communities.

- As early as 1983, the National Telemedia Council
(*www.nationaltelemediacouncil.org*) began
working with teachers to introduce media
literacy in the classroom. In 1995, it organized
the first National Media Education Conference.

- Center for Media Literacy (*www.medialit.org*)
provides other media-literacy links, an online

catalog of resources for parents and educators, as well as seminars and workshops for educators and activists. Specifically, "Assignment: Media Literacy" is their comprehensive new curriculum resource designed to strengthen media-literacy and communication skills. The organization has also developed twelve "Media Literacy Workshop Kits" for teachers, community leaders, parenting groups, and church or synagogue instructors. The kit includes handouts, videos, lesson and activity plans, and manuals and background material for teachers.

- Media Education Foundation (*www.mediaed .org*) was founded in 1981 by Sut Jhally, professor of communications at the University of Massachusetts. This organization is "devoted to bolstering media literacy in the face of a communications landscape increasingly dominated by corporate media giants and multinational mergers." It now produces and distributes more than forty educational videos, many with accompanying study guides.
- Citizens for Media Literacy (*http://main.nc.us/cml*) "advocates media literacy as a tool to produce engaged citizens who will actively question corporate power and consumer culture."
- Media Literacy Review (*http://interact.uoregon .edu/MediaLit/mlr/home*), based at the University of Oregon, is a key source for online resources on media literacy and has links to media-literacy organizations, lesson plans, training programs, and events worldwide.

- New Mexico Media Literacy Project (*www.nmmlp.org*), directed by Bob McCannon, has developed and implemented an effective media-literacy curriculum in New Mexico that is now used in thousands of schools worldwide. It offers several products in addition to that curriculum: a video entitled *Just Do Media Literacy* and several CD ROMs, including *Understanding Media* and *Media Literacy: Reversing Addiction in Our Compulsive Culture*. NMMLP also gives workshops, presentations, and training sessions to all interested.
  - Project Look Sharp (*www.ithaca.edu/looksharp*) is an initiative to promote and support the integration of media literacy into classroom curricula at all grade levels and instructional areas as well as to evaluate the effectiveness of media-literacy education in the schools.
- Support, support, support! By joining and donating money to organizations that advocate socially responsible media, you empower them to speak on your behalf, relaying a united and powerful message to those who can make lasting changes, small or large. Although you could support the groups above, here are some others that are also worthy of your membership, input, and financial support:
  - Fairness and Accuracy in Reporting [FAIR] (*www.fair.org*) is committed to monitoring the media and incidents of media bias.
  - Citizens Coalition for Responsible Media (*www.fairpress.org*) is a media watchdog. By closely following critical issues, monitoring

media performance, and through grassroots activism, using the powers of purchase and persuasion, they strive to (1) expose media bias and fraud, (2) bring pressure to bear for media reform, and (3) direct others toward more reliable news sources when faced with cases of continued bias, inaccuracy, or unfairness.

- Independent Media Center (*www.indymedia.org*) is a collective of independent media organizations and hundreds of journalists that offers grassroots, noncorporate coverage.
- AlterNet (*www.AlterNet.org*), a project of Indy-Media, provides a mix of news, opinion, and investigative journalism on a variety of important issues relevant to society's future.
- New Dimensions Radio (*www.newdimensions.org*), an independent, listener-supported producer and distributor of public radio, shortwave, and Internet programs, is dedicated to presenting a diversity of views from many traditions and cultures.
- Truth Out (*www.truthout.org*) is an alternative news source providing critical news and commentary on world events.
- The TV Turnoff Network (*www.tvturnoff.org*) is a nonprofit organization that encourages children and adults to watch much less television in order to promote healthier lives and communities.

● Support, either with your time or your checkbook, other groups that advocate for responsible media, and get others in the community to do the same.

Examples include Children Now, Junior League, PTA, and the Center for Media Education.

- If you are a member of a congregation, approach church or synagogue leaders and discuss ways you can help support or organize campaigns that actively promote responsible use of the media.
- Get together with key players in your community to organize and promote a "Turn off the TV Week" or participate in the national Turn Off the TV Week, held annually in April (*www.tvturnoff.org*).

Can you imagine if we could not only raise our children to become masters of their own choices so that they make decisions which honor sound values but could also replace harmful external messages with positive ones? This is a dream we can and will realize. And when we reach that dream, our everyday heroes will live out their lives in a heroic world.

Conclusion

Now we're ready to send our children on their journey toward heroism. Although it may seem like we have our work cut out for us, raising children to be everyday heroes is actually much easier than the conventional parenting practices we've grown accustomed to. Our old ways leave us fumbling around in darkness, hoping against hope that our kids will grow up sane and whole. But like shooting into a barrel of fish, parenting by command is a hit-or-miss proposition at best. Sometimes it works and sometimes it doesn't. Sadly, the times that it fails us are often the times success matters most. On the other hand, parenting that inspires the hero within is a ten-million-watt lantern that lights our way, giving us the clarity that has escaped generations of parents before us.

More reasons exist for us to take on the challenge to raise a family, and therefore a world, of heroes than to stand idly by and continue on the same charted course:

- We'll see an end to the conflict and hostility many families endure.
- Relationships with our children will become loving, peaceful, and personally fulfilling.
- Because it doesn't require perfection in parenting, this approach is less demanding and stressful. Once

they experience child-rearing that guides them respectfully toward self-mastery, heroes in the making recognize our mistakes for what they are. Without that added stress, parenting becomes a joy rather than a burden.

- The positive effects on our children and the family as a whole occur so quickly that parenting becomes a more gratifying experience within a matter of weeks, creating more motivation to implement parenting changes confidently and consistently. Going back to the old ways will seem the more arduous and unpalatable choice.

- Giving up is not an option. It's never too late to bring out the inner hero in a child. I've seen as dramatic a change in my teenagers as I have in my younger children.

- This is perhaps the first time our children have been offered another way of making choices and gaining acceptance. And when they see this new, self-directed decision-making process for what it is, they have no problem abandoning their old externally directed ways as flawed.

- Children feel better being guided rather than managed or controlled. They feel better without the power struggles, the vague and ever-shifting limits, and the need for others to direct their choices and lives.

- It feels wonderful to have faith in our children. And because of that faith, we'll feel perfectly at ease delegating much of the responsibility for growing up well to them. Parenting won't be nearly as burdensome or time-consuming.

- When we parent our children to nurture their heroism, we become so aware of the way they make choices, the way they choose to be guided, and how they gain acceptance that we begin to observe the same in our friends, our neighbors, our relatives, characters on television programs or movies—and eventually ourselves. From that awareness, we too will grow more and more self-directed. We too will develop the inner strength that will bring out the hero in us.

These are personal reasons for becoming a parent devoted to raising heroes. But don't take my word for it. I challenge you to try an exercise for two weeks. For that time period, eliminate all directives and negatives and try to deliver logical or natural consequences as your primary discipline strategy. You'll be impressed with the results in both your family and your children—inner strength that pervades the soul of the family and each of its members. That said, both parenthood and childhood become our great gifts, struggles and all.

Before us stands an opportunity we can't ignore—the opportunity to uncover the treasure that lies in every child. As parents, it is up to us to be the catalysts for change, the activists dedicated to helping children reach their full potential, the leaders who will fill the world with self-reliant, responsible, self-confident, compassionate, and moral heroes.

By daring to wander outside our white picket fences, past the limits of the stability, security, and anonymity they embrace, together we can raise a heroic world. To inspire that leap of faith, we must ask ourselves this:

Do we continue to regard our young as needy and incorrigible, or do we have faith in them for the first time in human history? Poised on the brink of peace or strife, the outcome hinges completely on the attitude we decide to adopt. We are the parents of our world's future, for we alone can choose which path humanity will take. And because we love our children so dearly, we *will* choose wisely.

About the Author

Dr. Elisa Medhus is a veteran physician who built and operated a successful private medical practice in Houston, Texas, for thirteen years. Her busy practice served thousands of families. She is also the mother of five children ages nine through nineteen, some of whom have special challenges like Tourette's Syndrome, Attention Deficit Disorder, learning differences, and Obsessive Compulsive Disorder.

With over nineteen years of experience parenting her own children, several years of experience home-schooling her children, and thirteen years of experience as a family physician, Dr. Medhus is uniquely qualified to address the concerns of parents.

Over the last several years, Dr. Medhus began to notice that children, including her own, seem more influenced by their peers and the pop culture than by their parents. Seeing the negative effect this has on families, children, schools, and communities, she embarked on a lengthy interview process to try to determine the cause of this destructive phenomenon. Based on the interview results and her own experience and expertise, she decided that by giving children the tools they need to make responsible choices — choices that are governed by their sense of right and wrong rather than by their need for approval — these influences would no longer hold such power over them. And then parents would no longer be obsolete; children would grow to think for themselves; and the world would become a safer, saner place. In her first book, *Raising Children Who Think for Themselves*, Dr. Medhus gives a detailed explanation of this concept and provides practical solutions for raising self-directed children and, therefore, creating a self-directed world. The book has earned numerous prestigious awards, including the Parents' Choice Award, the National Parenting Center Award, and the National Parenting Publications Award. It is widely available in bookstores and from online booksellers and has been translated into four languages. In her second book, *Hearing Is Believing: How Words Can Make or Break Our Kids*, Dr. Medhus argues that even seemingly harmless phrases such as "You're such a good girl" can encourage children to become approval-seekers, thwart their ability to reason, or both. Over time, these children become less inclined to trust their parents' guidance and internalize their values. Exposing potentially harmful words and phrases — many that may surprise readers — this book suggests language changes that are simple to implement and keep up.

In high demand as a keynote speaker and as a guest on television and radio, Dr. Medhus regularly discusses the issues and problems facing today's families.

Bibliography

Introduction

Public Agenda. "A Lot Easier Said Than Done: Parents Talk About Raising Children in Today's America" (2002). www.publicagenda.org/specials/parents/parents.htm.

Chapter 2

Auffermann, Kyra. "What's Up: Students Continue Volunteering, Even When It's Not Required" (25 April 2003). www.andovertownsman.com/.

Berliner, David. *The Manufactured Crisis: Myths, Fraud, and Attack on America's Public Schools*. Reading, Mass.: Addison-Wesley, 2000.

Digital Research, Inc. "Company News" (1999). www.digitalresearch.com/.

Howe, Neil, and William Strauss. *Millennials Rising: The Next Great Generation*. New York: Vintage Books, 2000.

Parent-Teen News Updates. "Parents and Kids: Nickelodeon-Time Magazine Survey" (2 August 2002). www.parent-teen.com/news.html.

Schneider, Barbara, and David Stevenson. *The Ambitious Generation: American's Teenagers, Motivated But Directionless*. New Haven, Conn.: Yale University Press, 1999.

Sung, H. H., A. M. Morrison, G.-S. Hong, and J. T. O'Leary. "The Effects of Household and Trip Characteristics on Trip Types: A Consumer Behavioral Approach for Segmenting the U.S. Domestic Leisure Travel Market." *Journal of Hospitality and Tourism Research* 25, no. 1 (2001): 46–68.

USA Weekend. "Survey of Teens" (1999). www.usaweekend.com/.

Vasquez, Gaddi. "Peace Corp Online: Peace Corp News" (26 March 2003). www.peacecorpsonline.org/.

Weintraub, Aileen, and Pamela Morse. "The National Service Year in Review" (2001). www.lifetimeofservice.org/.

Zollo, Peter. *Wise Up to Teens: Insights into Marketing and Advertising to Teenagers*. Ithaca, N.Y.: New Strategist Publications, 1999.

Chapter 3

Furedi, Frank. *Paranoid Parenting: Why Ignoring the Experts May Be Best for Your Child*. Chicago: Chicago Review Press, 2002.

Howe, Neil, and William Strauss. *Millennials Rising: The Next Great Generation*. New York: Vintage Books, 2000.

Kindlon, Daniel J. *Too Much of a Good Thing: Raising Children of Character in an Indulgent Age*. New York: Hyperion, 2001.

Public Agenda. "A Lot Easier Said Than Done: Parents Talk About Raising Children in Today's America" (2002). www.publicagenda.org/specials/parents/parents.htm.

Chapter 4

The Character Counts! Coalition. "The Ethics of American Youth, 2002 Report Card: Survey Documents Decade of Moral Deterioration." Josephson Institute of Ethics. www.josephsoninstitute.org/Survey2002/survey2002-pressrelease.htm.

Chatterjee, Sumana. "Young Americans' Drug Use Spikes." *Houston Chronicle*, 6 September 2002.

Farkas, Steve, and Jean Johnson. "Aggravating Circumstances: A Status Report on Rudeness in America." Public Agenda (2002). www.publicagenda.org/.

Four Nations Child Policy Network. "Youth Crime Research and Statistics" (2002). www.childpolicy.org/.

Furedi, Frank. *Paranoid Parenting: Why Ignoring the Experts May Be Best for Your Child*. Chicago: Chicago Review Press, 2002.

Harris County Psychiatric Center. "HCPC Offers Tips to Recognize, Handle Childhood Depression." *Texas Medical Center News* 21, no. 15 (15 August 1999). www.tmc.edu/tmcnews/08_15_99/page_09.html.

Hornbeck, David, and the Task Force on Education of Young Adolescents. *Turning Points: Preparing American Youth for the Twenty-first Century: The Report of the Task Force on Education of Young Adolescents*. New York: The Carnegie Council on Adolescent Development, 1989.

Howe, Neil, and Bill Strauss. *Thirteenth Gen: Abort, Retry, Ignore, Fail?* New York: Random, Vintage, 1993.

Kindlon, Daniel J. *Too Much of a Good Thing: Raising Children of Character in an Indulgent Age*. New York: Hyperion, 2001.

Luthar, Suniya S., and Bronwyn E. Becker. "Privileged But Pressured: A Study of Affluent Youth." *Child Development* 73, no. 5 (September/October 2002): 1593–1610.

Mogel, Wendy. *The Blessing of a Skinned Knee: Using Jewish Teachings to Raise Self-Reliant Children*. New York: Penguin USA, 2001.

MyGroupHealth. "Test Your Knowledge of Teen Drugs" (2004). www.ghc.org/features/.

Public Agenda. "A Lot Easier Said Than Done: Parents Talk About Raising Children in Today's America" (2002). www.publicagenda.org/specials/parents/parents.htm.

Steyer, James P. *The Other Parent: The Inside Story of the Media's Effect on Our Children*. New York: Atria Books, 2002.

Substance Abuse and Mental Health Administration. "Annual Household Survey Finds Millions of Americans in Denial about Drug Abuse" (2001). U.S. Department of Health and Human Services. www.samhsa.gov/news/content/2001nhsda.htm.

Chapter 5

Carroll, Joseph. "Parent/Teen Relations: Where's the Grief?" 2000 Gallup Youth Survey. www.gallup.com/.

Haag, Pamela. *Voices of a Generation: Teenage Girls on Sex, School, and Self*. Washington, D.C.: American Association of University Women, 1999.

Kaiser Family Foundation and Nickelodeon. "Talking with Kids About Tough Issues" (2001). www.talkingwithkids.org/.

Kindlon, Daniel J. *Too Much of a Good Thing: Raising Children of Character in an Indulgent Age*. New York: Hyperion, 2001.

Kittredge, Karen, and Alice R. McCarthy. "Peer Pressure: Today's Youth Face Pressures from Many Unprecedented Factors, Not Only Peers." *The Brown University Child and Adolescent Behavior Letter* 16, no. 6 (June 2000). www.childresearch.net/cybrary/news/200006.htm.

Kohn, Alfie. *The Schools Our Children Deserve*. New York: Houghton Mifflin, 2000.

Putnam, Robert D. *Bowling Alone : The Collapse and Revival of American Community*. New York: Simon & Schuster, 2001.

Chapter 8

Covey, Stephen R. *The Seven Habits of Highly Effective Families*. New York: Golden Books Adult Publishing, 1998.

Chapter 9

McGraw, Jay. *Life Strategies for Teens*. New York: Fireside, 2000.

Chapter 10

Myers, Isabel Briggs. Myers-Briggs Type Indicator (MBTI). www.personalitypage.com/.

Norman, Jane. "Building Effective Youth-Adult Partnerships." *Transitions* 14, no. 1 (October 2001). www.advocatesforyouth.org/publications/transitions/transitions1401.htm.

Chapter 11

Kilpatrick, William, and Gregory and Suzanne M. Wolfe. *Books That Build Character: A Guide to Teaching Your Child Moral Values through Stories*. New York: Simon & Schuster, Touchstone Books, 1994.

Lesko, Wendy. *Maximum Youth Involvement: The Complete Gameplan for Community Action* (2003). www.youth activism.com/myitoc.htm.

Rosen, Elana Yonah, Arleta Paulin Quesada, and Sue Lockwood Summers. *Changing the World through Media Education: A New Media Education Curriculum*. Golden, Colo.: Fulcrum Publishing, Just Think Foundation, 1998.

Steyer, James P. *The Other Parent: The Inside Story of the Media's Effect on Our Children*. New York: Atria Books, 2002.

OTHER BOOKS FROM
BEYOND WORDS PUBLISHING, INC.

Raising Children Who Think for Themselves
Author: Elisa Medhus, M.D.
$14.95, softcover

Raising Children Who Think for Themselves offers a new approach to parenting that has the power to reverse the trend of external direction in children—that tendency to make decisions based on outside influences—and to help parents bring up empathetic, self-confident, moral, independent thinkers. Filled with real-life examples, humorous anecdotes, and countless interviews with parents, children, and teachers, this book identifies the five essential qualities of self-directed children, outlines the seven strategies necessary for parents to develop these qualities in their children, and offers solutions to nearly one hundred child-raising challenges.

Guided Imagery for Healing Children and Teens
Wellness Through Visualization
Author: Ellen Curran
$14.95, softcover

The naturally rich imaginations of children are one of the best resources for healing or helping children through difficult times. This book explains how the extraordinary technique of guided imagery can be used as part of a wellness plan for ill or injured children. It introduces the parent/caregiver to the philosophy and science of mind-body medicine and imagery and can also be used by healthcare workers, school nurses, home health nurses, physicians, and wellness practitioners.

Nurture Your Child's Gift

Inspired Parenting

Author: Caron Goode, Ed.D.

$14.95, softcover

Nurture Your Child's Gift helps parents create space and support for their children to recognize their personal vision and make their unique contribution in life. This book answers parents' questions, such as "How can I help my children find a direction for their lives? How can I motivate them? How can I help them be happy?" Goode explains the three building blocks for children to successfully achieve their life vision—esteem, empowerment, and expression—and shows parents how to help bring these forth.

Believe to Achieve

See the Invisible, Do the Impossible

Author: Howard "H" White

$17.95, hardcover

Howard "H" White tells us: *Extraordinary people are simply ordinary people on fire with desire*—and he knows. As Nike, Inc.'s liaison for athletes such as Michael Jordan and Charles Barkley, "H" has had plenty of experience with superstars. But he didn't start there. He has known extraordinary people his whole life, from his family and friends to his coaches and teachers. All along the way Howard has met people who opened his eyes to his own abilities, and he's spent his life doing the same for others.

Full of behind-the-scenes moments with favorite athletes as well as funny anecdotes, *Believe to Achieve* is an exuberant collection of wisdom that will help you recognize the potential in yourself and see the path to success. It's a handbook for all people who have a goal they don't know how to reach or who want to help others discover their gifts.

Nurturing Your Child with Music

How Sound Awareness Creates Happy, Smart, and Confident Children

Author: John M. Ortiz, Ph.D.

$14.95, softcover

Author and psychomusicologist Dr. John Ortiz says that we have "just begun to tap into the powers behind the timeless element of sound," and in his book *Nurturing Your Child with Music*, Dr. Ortiz allows the readers to discover those musical powers through and with their children. Designed for parents who take an active interest in their children's lives, this book offers a number of creative methods through which families can initiate, enhance, and maintain happy, relaxed, and productive home environments. *Nurturing Your Child with Music* includes easy-to-do exercises and fun activities to bring music and sound into parenting styles and family life. The book provides music menus and sample "days of sound" to use during the prenatal, newborn, preschool, and school-age phases. Dr. Ortiz shares how we can keep our family "in tune" and create harmony in our homes by inviting music and sound into our daily dance of life.

Teach Only Love

The Twelve Principles of Attitudinal Healing

Author: Gerald G. Jampolsky, M.D.

$12.95, softcover

From best-selling author Dr. Gerald Jampolsky comes a revised and expanded version of one of his classic works, based on *A Course in Miracles*. In 1975, Dr. Jampolsky founded the Center for Attitudinal Healing, a place where children and adults with life-threatening illnesses could practice peace of mind as an instrument of spiritual transformation and inner healing—practices that soon evolved into an approach to life with profound benefits for everyone. This book explains the twelve principles developed at the Center, all of which are based on the healing power of love, forgiveness, and oneness. They provide a powerful guide that allows all of us to heal our relationships and bring peace and harmony to every aspect of our lives.

Forgiveness
The Greatest Healer of All
Author: Gerald G. Jampolsky, M.D.
Foreword: Neale Donald Walsch
$12.95, softcover

Forgiveness: The Greatest Healer of All is written in simple, down-to-earth language. It explains why so many of us find it difficult to forgive and why holding on to grievances is really a decision to suffer. The book describes what causes us to be unforgiving and how our minds work to justify this. It goes on to point out the toxic side effects of being unforgiving and the havoc it can play on our bodies and on our lives. But above all, it leads us to the vast benefits of forgiving.

The author shares powerful stories that open our hearts to the miracles which can take place when we truly believe that no one needs to be excluded from our love. Sprinkled throughout the book are Forgiveness Reminders that may be used as daily affirmations supporting a new life free of past grievances.

Girls Who Rocked the World
Heroines from Sacagawea to Sheryl Swoopes
Author: Amelie Welden
$8.95, softcover

Girls Who Rocked the World is the follow-up to *Girls Know Best*. Both books encourage girls to believe in themselves and go for their dreams. *Girls Who Rocked the World* tells the stories of thirty-five real girls, past and present, from all around the world, who achieved amazing feats and changed history *before reaching their twenties*. Included are well-known girls like Helen Keller and Sacagawea as well as many often-overlooked heroines such as Joan of Arc, Phillis Wheatley, and Wang Yani. Interspersed along with the stories of heroines are photos and writings of real girls from all over America answering the question, "How do I plan to rock the world?" By highlighting the goals and dreams of these girls, the book links these historical heroines to girls today who will be the next ones to rock the world!

Boys Know It All
Wise Thoughts and Wacky Ideas from Guys Like You
Editor: Marianne Monson
$8.95, softcover

Stereotypes and the pressure to conform often smother the creativity of boys and leave their fresh, original ideas unheard. *Boys Know It All* is a place where boys can speak their piece about what it is to be a boy. Boys, ages six to sixteen, have written chapters offering helpful hints for tough situations like talking to girls and surviving older siblings, while others toss out ways to fill free time creatively like inventing your own family traditions and taking care of pets. This is a fun book that also tackles serious issues about growing up male in America. Boys will enjoy reading it and will even get excited about learning and trying new things.

To order or to request a catalog, contact
Beyond Words Publishing, Inc.
20827 N.W. Cornell Road, Suite 500
Hillsboro, OR 97124-9808
503-531-8700

You can also visit our Web site at *www.beyondword.com* or e-mail us at *info@beyondword.com*.

Beyond Words Publishing, Inc.

OUR CORPORATE MISSION
Inspire to Integrity

OUR DECLARED VALUES
We give to all of life as life has given us.
We honor all relationships.
Trust and stewardship are integral to fulfilling dreams.
Collaboration is essential to create miracles.
Creativity and aesthetics nourish the soul.
Unlimited thinking is fundamental.
Living your passion is vital.
Joy and humor open our hearts to growth.
It is important to remind ourselves of love.